# The School of Flaunt Handbook

by

**Alexandra Smythe**
**and**
**Cate Clarke**

TELEMACHUS
PRESS

**The School of Flaunt Handbook**

Cover designed by Trans World Productions Inc. with assistance from Telemachus Press, LLC

Cover art copyright © iStockPhoto #6942314

Interior art copyright © Joel Woodard Interior Design, LLC
www.joelwoodard.com

Published by Telemachus Press, LLC
http://www.telemachuspress.com

Visit the author's website at http://www.schoolofflaunt.com

ISBN # 978-1-937387-17-4 eBook
ISBN# 978-1-937387-18-1 Paperback
ISBN# 978-1-937387-19-8 Hardback

Version 2011.11.28

Printed in the United States of America
10 9 8 7 6 5 4 3 2 1

# Dedications

*We dedicate this book to those who exemplify the highest of School of Flaunt standards.*

*Audrey Hepburn*
*Cary Grant*
*Princess Grace of Monaco*
*Jacqueline Bouvier Kennedy Onassis*
*Ivanka Trump*
*The Duke and Duchess of Cambridge*

*We also want to acknowledge our husbands, who have always treated us like queens!*

# About the Authors

## Biography of Cate Cadbury-Clarke

CATE CADBURY WAS born in the Cotswold's, the only daughter of a Chocolate Baron, Cleland Cadbury and his lovely wife, Clarissa. Cate spent her very early childhood as many British upper class children do, replete with nannies, nurses and doting parents with lots of candy. Oddly, Cate has perfect teeth!

At a very young age she developed a keen interest in everything American and would skip and whistle through the house to Yankee Doodle Dandy! Cate started to beg her parents to let her visit her "Yank" relatives in the states. Finally Cleland and Clarissa acquiesced and sent her for that visit.

This was a major life changer, for at the end of the summer Cate asked her parents if she could stay in the states, and promised that she would attend a posh private school. Of course it had an equestrienne training facility which she knew would make her Mummy happy, for the love of Dressage does run in the family. But it still took many phone calls, tears and cajoling for Cleland and Clarissa to finally say yes.

Alas a few years later, her driver's license and new Mustang convertible turned her into a total Yank. To her parents chagrin she wanted to attend an American university to study art and design. Now she was a Yank through and through and most vestiges of her British background were gone including her Brit accent which was very upsetting to Clarissa. One thing remained though her love of scones and clotted cream!

Cate would return to England for visits on a frequent basis and always used this as an excuse to travel Europe too. This was how she met Alexandra Braithwaite.

The story of their meeting goes down in the history books of the Paris Ritz Carlton! Alexandra Braithwaite sashayed into the Tea Room of the Ritz with her 747 crew. They had been bumped from the large hotel chain where they usually spent their layovers and were "upgraded" to the Ritz Carlton. When Cate watched these people, she was intrigued by the slick uniforms and attractive men and women entering the lobby. She asked one bright woman who they worked for, and the rest is history!

Cate and Alexandra spent the morning chatting and drinking "Crew Tea" in the lobby bar as the Ritz staff snapped photos of the two young beauties celebrating and entertaining their fellow guests at the hotel. Unfortunately, these photos have since disappeared after having spent many years on the walls of the lobby bar. However, the senior staff who are still working at the Ritz remember the twosome oh so well, and they still look forward to their arrival together. More importantly though, this chance French meeting is how the "School of Flaunt" was born!

Postscript:
Cate Cadbury-Clarke did indeed join Alexandra and became a Flight Attendant with The Major International Carrier. So, prior to Private Jets coming into vogue, Alexandra and Cate traveled in the First Class World, meeting and greeting the top celebrities, politicians who would

become Presidents, nouveau riche, and yes the occasional Headline Grabbing Criminal in Handcuffs! What the two ladies viewed and experienced became fodder for the School of Flaunt, so much money, such bad taste and such poor manners. Something had to be done! Hence, The School of Flaunt Handbook was born.

Cate has since become an American Citizen and resides in the U.S. with her family, and is in constant contact with her BFF, Alexandra.


## Biography of Alexandra Braithwaite-Smythe

ALEXANDRA BRAITHWAITE-SMYTHE learned the lessons of good taste from her family. As her mother, Mrs. Cornelius Braithwaite, often told her from the time that she was a young girl, "you can always tell the *nouveau riche*. They have to tell you about how much money they spent on everything. Alexandra's mother would continue with the comment: "it is so *déclassé*. You automatically know they do not come from old money."

Remember, "old money, quiet money" have their own language. As her Great Aunt said when she was throwing a social soiree, whether a small children's birthday party or an event for 100's and wanted it splashed across the society pages, "It is not what you say but how you say it. Even if you are only having a small birthday party it should always be written up as a grand affair." This thought would remain with her forever.

As Alexandra watched her mother navigate through the Ladies Symphony Club, President of this and that organization and always politically active; she knew how to move in the very best circles. Starting out, at a young age, it was a must in her high school to join a Sorority, so naturally she did. Then to be a mover and shaker in college again you needed to be in a college Sorority. So she sought out the best one on campus to pledge, known for not only their beauty but brains. Both would open those social doors and also prove to be beneficial later in life.

After graduating from college with a number of honorariums; Alexandra could have gone in a number of directions. But she was a free spirit and as a lark one day, she decided to become an International Flight Attendant for a major airline, and we might add here that Mrs. Cornelius Braithwaite did not approve! As she told her daughter, "why do you think we spent all of that money on your college education? What will our friends think?" Surprisingly her father pulled her aside and said, "Don't worry about your Mother. I'll handle this; you go and have a good time." And that is what she did!

Postscript:
Alexandra followed in the family footsteps and became active in charitable groups, clubs and Boards, but from her adventures and experiences when she saw the "nouveau riche" and "not so rich," up close and personal, she knew they needed her help. This was the birth of the School of Flaunt with her co-writer and partner in "good taste," Cate Clarke.

# The School of Flaunt Handbook

# Table of Contents

# Introduction

YES, WE HAVE entered the 21st century and where are the majority of you? Are you still stuck in the nightmarish taste from the 80s or 90s? Then, this primer is for you!

Your income or net worth mean nothing when it comes to taste! As we walk the local shopping centers and streets of large cities, mid-size towns and out in the country we are aghast at how all of you are dressing, eating, talking, living and even how you are walking. Do you resemble someone in a "fast food" ad, slurping a soft drink, eating with one hand and not even thinking of using a napkin? Well, we are here to offer you advice, guidance, and even sordid stories to help you get out of the ugly, daily rut of tasteless living that screams, "Tacky, no class, no money, no breeding!"

Ah, and here you are saying to yourself at this very moment, "They're not talking about me, but it could be my neighbor, friend or relative who could use this advice." We are here to tell you that you better look into the mirror and around your home before you put down this book! In fact, you should run to the mirror right now because we can most assuredly guess that you are not in the .01 percent that has good taste! You can spend countless hours in front of the flat screen watching reality TV about real life, tawdry housewives and their crazy families, "Survivor," or, heaven forbid, Jerry Springer and his tacky guests. But all of these hours, which are considered the

American pastime called watching TV, count for nothing. Think: American Idol is giving you a major IDOL THUMBS DOWN!

Now, you might be offended by this bluntness and we certainly do not want that to be our message. We are only here to help you! We would prefer that you be the beacon of good taste, refinement, and elegance that people want to know and associate with. This is called savoir faire (pronounced savwaar fair), and you will know it thoroughly by the time you have finished this book.

So you think that sounds boring and stuffy. You'd rather be that dull knife in the drawer, throwing down a beer after riding your dirt bike. Well, people, that is going to get you nowhere and, in fact, you will be the one who is boring!

Our goal here is to open doors of opportunity for you, and they don't come from a dirt bike background. We want you to be sophisticated, poised and interesting! Why? Because everyone is drawn to the well-mannered. So, our first bit of advice that you can "take to the bank" is that people gravitate to others that they would like to emulate or be with. And here is the really good news—you don't need a vault full of money to draw people to you. If you follow our advice, your entire life could change for the better.

This is where the School of Flaunt handbook comes in. We will teach you all the fine points of how to dress, walk, talk, play, live, and, yes, be interesting to all. You will have the knowledge of the ways of society and know how to conduct yourself with sophistication and polish. This is savoir vivre (pronounced savwaar veevra). You now are a student in the School of Flaunt and, after reading this book, you will qualify for your Graduation Diploma. **Go to: www. schooloflflaunt.com and click on PRODUCTS, to order your personal graduation diploma.** Congratulations are in order to each and every one of you that wants to improve your image and life.

Now, students of The School of Flaunt, please pick up your yellow marker, have a pen and pad at the ready for notes, and, trust us, there are no Cliff notes to cheat with! Flaunt is all in the details.

Let us begin …

## LESSON ONE:
## Wardrobe

"From Runway to Reality"

GOOD TASTE IS just a Black American Express Card away ...
we can hear your minds ticking right now. What is a Black American
Express Card? You've never heard of one; let alone seen one. Well,
that is probably because only a limited number of them exist in the
entire world. Your credit limit is in the millions. So if someone flashes
one of those little beauties, you know that you are in the company of a
true School of Flaunt devotee! This is Black Stealth Buying at its best!

But we digress, students. Let us get on to your first lesson:
Wardrobe. Remember, the quality of your clothes should reflect the
quality of your life! Surround yourself with quality, and good taste
will follow. However, if you have no taste and have not been given that
wonderful attribute from birth, (which most of you have not,) and
you do not recognize the best in the business, please put yourselves
in the hands of professionals. These Guides of Glam are referred to as
"professional wardrobe consultants," and we will now refer to them
as your PWC. A PWC will easily guide you through the intimidating
maze of the plush-carpeted land known as the "Designer Floor." And,
believe it or not, in most top establishments, there is no additional
charge for this. Do not be confused. A stylist is paid handsomely for
these services ... think Red Carpet Glam.

Let us ask you, students, do you really think that the ultra rich, or most celebrities, dress themselves? When they do, oh please! It can be pitiful. Look at some of the outrageous outfits of poor taste that they come up with. So now we want you to think: Tim Gunn, Anna Wintour, Rachel Zoe or Carson Kressley. If your PWC isn't personal friends with one of them, or at least displays the same impeccable taste as the aforementioned, then get rid of him or her immediately and demand a new one! Remember, these guides of taste and Flaunt Fashionistas are available at the best of shops. Try Barney's, Bendel's, Bergdorf's, Prada, Hermés or Neiman Marcus! No more fashion faux pas (French for mistake) for our School of Flaunt (SOF) students, whom we will now refer to as SOF'ers. You must develop a sense of style, and this only comes through practice!

Can we talk here? Silhouettes, silhouettes—so many to choose from and so little time; Armani Black Label, Dolce & Gabbana, Oscar de la Renta, the late Alexander McQueen, Chanel, Ralph Lauren, Vera Wang, Valentino, and Stella McCartney to name a few! And then there is the new kid on the block, Jason Wu. Remember his name. He is now designing for our First Lady, Michelle Obama, and you can even purchase his clothes off the rack, a School of Flaunt seal of approval for his feminine designs! Last, but always a fashion staple for any woman, should be a dress from Diane Von Furstenberg. So easy to throw on, and when combined with a great pair of shoes and some jewelry, you can go from work to dinner.

Remember, "from runway to reality," as designer Michael Kors said. Please, students, start checking out those couture fashions, because you will be wearing a more subdued version in the coming season and, at the very least, you should know what colors will be big! Poorly made and ill-fitting clothing should now give you a headache—actually, more like a migraine!

Are you fiscally challenged? Well, dear students, here is a **Flaunt Fiscal Tip**: To save some money—alterations! Yes, you can take a less expensive outfit and, with some good alterations by your seamstress or tailor, turn that dress, pair of slacks, or jacket into something that people will think is much more costly because it fits so well.

Think of turning a Banana Republic suit into an Armani fit. Well, that might be pushing it, but you get our point.

Speaking of fit, there is a rule to proportion, called "the Golden Ratio," which will give you that Flaunt Figure. Never heard of it? Well, it has been used for thousands of years in paintings, architecture, and yes, even in clothing. You will have to research this topic, as it is far too complicated to address in a few sentences, but let's try to simplify it. Why does a neckline, such as a turtleneck or boatneck, make some women look like a chubby sports mascot? (Think the "Philly Fanatic" here.) Now visualize a shirt or sweater with a V neckline that is slightly in line with your underarm. (Think Heidi Klum here). Are you visualizing, students? If you still don't have the picture, think about this: a lower V-shaped neckline automatically draws the eye down to your cleavage (obviously), but, hopefully, the eye is also drawn to the thinner part of your torso. We can only pray now! If that happens, then, voila, you have a slimmer look. (The "big" problem of too much cleavage will be addressed later in this lesson.)

Continuing on with proportions, let's talk skirt lengths that hit you in the middle of your calf. Dowdy looking? Yes! Total Flaunt Failure? Yes! Students, this length is only acceptable with a pair of high-heeled, leather boots, preferably Ferragamos. Try putting that skirt at the middle of your knee and see how it enhances your legs. Now think fatty knee caps and covering them up! Who wants to show off those things? So you are short or have the perfect knees—then put that skirt length above your knee. It is all about the ratio. Lastly, lets talk minis, as in skirt length. If you don't have a great set of legs and are over 40, don't even think about it! All we can picture is spider veins and those plump knee caps. Oh, that thought makes us cringe! Valium! Where is the valium? (Please consult Lesson Fourteen about cosmetic surgery.)

Just remember, students, that because something is deemed the latest in style, that doesn't mean that it is for you. We are all different heights, weights, and skin tones. If purple is big for the season and you look like a dried out plum in it then just add a little purple in your choice of shoes or a handbag. Forget it next to your face. That goes for lipstick too! Don't get sucked in with those ads in Vogue magazine or someone dancing around on television telling you that you simply must be wearing this color! (Consult Lesson Two for makeup tips.)

Lest we forget one small detail: we know you were tempted to purchase that beautiful evening gown with the train. Think about when you are not on the "red carpet," your train trailing behind you through the muck and the mire. Ugly stains! How are you going to dance on the dance floor without either killing yourself or someone else when they step on your train? Headline in the NY Times: "Socialite in hospital after she trips on train when dancing." Just a thought, students.

****

Now, getting back to using your PWC (or professional guide of glam): let them help you pick the most attractive looks. Accessorize with Jimmy Choo, Manolo Blahnik, or red-soled Christian Louboutin shoes. Handbags from Michael Kors, Mark Jacobs, Chanel, Prada, Gucci, Bottega Veneta, Hermés, Judith Lieber, and Louis Vuitton will carry you through your busy new life! Oh, so many choices, and so little time to use them all. But it is always exciting to get out that bag or pair of shoes that you haven't seen for awhile. If you still look at them and have that initial feeling of, "I love you," your heart starts to race slightly, and you might even have a bead of perspiration on your upper lip, then you have chosen well.

For those of you who don't know this, handbags and shoes have always been considered little "status symbols," showing who has it and who doesn't. Frankly, we wouldn't consider them investments, but could your bag be a collectible? In 2007, Louis Vuitton, known as LV, produced a limited, "numbered," purse called the "Patchwork" bag. By limited, we mean that 24 bags were made from their former cruise lines collections. Yes, the LV staff went into their museum, selected 15 bags from former glory days, and made 24 new ones out of the 15. Was it that the bags were numbered, or their $45,000 price tag that made them sell out rapidly? Who knows? Who really cares? We just want one, too!

Then for total flaunt there is the Hermés "Birkin" bag, which normally retails for approximately $6,000 to $37,000. One was auctioned off at the Doyle New York auction in April of 2005 for $64,000. Why? Well, this little black-skinned crocodile beauty also had silver hardware, 14 carat white gold closure plates with 174 pave set diamonds, and 310 more diamonds on the lock. These diamonds weighed in at 14.11 carats. We think this bag would be considered both an investment and a collectible. One of our School of Flaunt idols, Princess Grace of Monaco, would have been proud since she helped put the Birkin bag on the list of things to have.

Just an explanation here: What does pave mean? If you answered, "Covering a street with paving," that is not what we were referring to. Correct answer: A setting of jewels placed closely together. (See Lesson Three about jewelry.)

And lastly, dear Judith Leiber. No grand dame of society should be without a JL bag! Consider possibly one of her most expensive, the Leiber Precious Rose, replete with diamonds and pink sapphires, sold for a small kingly ransom of $92,000. Makes our heads spin with the very thought of walking into the room with that in hand! Do we need to sit down and take a break? A moment of silence is recommended to acknowledge Judith and her lovely designs.

Oh, we can hear your little minds ticking now, thinking, "But I can't afford those name brand bags." Well, then remember this: if you are purchasing a less expensive bag, buy one that has very few exposed metal pieces, as these are always a hallmark of inferiority. Trust us on this. Remember the Birkin bag that we spoke about before, with its silver hardware? We'll repeat this one more time. Get a bag that shows almost no metal pieces on the exterior. To prove this point, buy that cheaper bag and then take it to Neiman Marcus and compare it to a true designer bag. The hardware on the less expensive bag will jump out at you like a dull penny! Ugly! SOF advice: Take it back immediately!

****

Now students, continuing on. We feel very strongly about buying good accessories. They can really add that little punch to your outfit, which may not be that pricey. When you add a wonderful belt, scarf, purse, or pair of shoes, it takes you to a different level. Remember fashion-statement students, classic and sophisticated, you are SOF material now.

Just a little aside here: ever think that a belt could cost $32,000? Selfridges & Co. from London created a man's 18 carat gold-studded belt on white leather, for the man who has everything. Unfortunately your waist had to be under 28 inches to get this price. For every additonal inch you had to be prepared to fork out another 800 £ English (as in +/- $1,600 dollars). Gucci, not wanting to be outdone, then came out with a monogrammed belt buckle made out of platinum, with 30 carats of diamonds, for a tidy little sum of $249,000, for an anonymous client. No, we are not kidding.

Students, one does not need to go to this extreme for a belt, but do consider an alligator or crocodile belt. They really do last a life time as long as you keep that waistline under control. Ladies, please do check out those Hermés scarves, as they are considered collect-ibles. They truly never go out of style. So, hopefully, you all now understand the importance of accessorizing well! A small note here: nothing says SOF better than using your Hermés scarf as a sling. If Princess Grace of Monaco could do this, surely you could. Just a sug-gestion, students.

Now, let us return to the topic of alligator and crocodile for just a moment. Alligator is the highest in quality, followed by crocodile, and then caiman, which is the lowest in quality. Please be ever-so careful when purchasing a handbag or wallet that claims to be made out of these products. It is easy to tell the differences between them.

Students, get out your yellow highlighter, then memorize the fol-lowing: alligator scales are flat with just a few fine crinkles along the edge, whereas crocodile scales have a small spot or dimple close to the edge. Caiman has a lot of lines and spots all through it.

Why do you want to know the difference? Because, alligator is softer and much more durable. It proves the old adage that you get what you pay for. What is the cost for enough alligator skin to make a small clutch or purse? Somewhere between $400 and $800, and then you have to add in the cost of making the item. Don't be taken in by embossed cow hide. The main clue is that the bag is probably only $19.95. Just understand what you are getting. Don't let that guy on the street sell you a fake! He'll be laughing all the way to the bank, and, unfortunately, everyone who knows the difference will be laughing at you. We do not want that to ever happen to our students. This is a total Flaunt Flop!

**Flaunt Fiscal Tip** for all of you want to be SOF'ers. There is an outlet center called Cabazon, outside of Palm Desert, CA. You will think you died and went to heaven! For example: Judith Leiber hand bags for one third of retail. So, even though we want you to start out using your PWC, when you feel that you can spread your wings and dress yourself with style it is time to start thinking, "No more retail!" If you can get a deal, work it!

**Flaunt Flash News**: Check out Shareen Vintage, in Los Angeles, or Chelsea, in NYC. Owner Shareen Mitchell was once an assistant to Polly Mellen at Vogue, so she knows what she is looking for. Shareen has an unbelievable stash of around 10,000 pieces for sale in LA, and is constantly restocking her store in NYC from the LA collection.

Shareen is reinventing vintage dresses from the likes of Oscar de la Renta and Carolina Herrera. Most are priced under $100. We can hear you now, saying, "Shut up!" Not one of our favorite expressions, but we know you are excited. This is not the Salvation Army here, students. But lest you forget, please develop some great style insight before you get adventuresome with vintage. You could end up being a total Flaunt Failure. We don't want that for you!

**\*\*\*\***

We must, at this point, bring up "haute couture." This is where "flaunt fashion" all starts! Most people don't have the bank account for these gowns, but at the very least you should know the term and what it means. In fashion terminology, these are garments that are completely custom made. When we say "completely," we don't mean, "off the rack and the dress is hemmed for you!" No! These are so custom that even the lining is made just for this garment and just for your body. The fabrics and embellishments, such as beads, lace, jewels, etc., are from the finest makers. You will have the best tailors, seamstresses, and craftsmen (yes, you did read plural there) assembling the pieces for this one-of-a-kind garment.

Couture chic clients can pay anywhere from a mere $25,000 for a couture gown to over a million dollars, or, very simply, whatever your pocketbook can afford. Don't think that this little number will be whipped up for you in a few days like a Hong Kong tailor making a suit. We are talking three to four months, at the very least, to get your finery! It is like joining a sorority. It is a private club for the very rich and very famous! Students, you don't just walk in and write the check. You must be invited by the director or directress of the house. The best way for this to happen is to be seen in Paris every January and July when the haute couture shows are held! At a minimum, know a few couture names to throw around, e.g., Adeline Andre, Versace Altelier, Zuhair Murad, Giorgio Armani, (who is still the king of haute couture pantsuits) Elie Saab, (known as ES to those in the know) and, always the tried and true grandest houses in Paris, Chanel and Dior. We wish you the best of luck on breaking into the Couture Club!

Just for your education, remember this: Chambre Syndicale de la Haute Couture. This is a division of the French Ministry of Industry, and a haute couturier is a designer who presides over the creation of hand-finished, made-to-order clothing, in a "laboratory" in Paris that employs at least 20 workers. The haute couturier must present a minimum of 25 ensembles (don't you love that word?) twice a year, in January and July, and construct a garment over the course of several fittings directly to the client's body or on a dress form replicating her physique. A couturier is simply someone who is sewing. Puh-leese, do not let anyone pull the wool over your eyes as to their status in the couture world! Haute couturier rules!

****

Now, we can hear you saying, "But I don't want to spend money on designer clothes." Here is our **Flaunt Secret**: As we said earlier, buy some good belts, high-end shoes, and handbags and add a few good pieces of jewelry. If you sneak in a fake diamond, you will have enough good pieces on your person that everyone will assume all is real. But heed us well, students: don't buy a fake Rolex. We know it is tempting, but anyone who owns a real one will know the difference. A real Rolex has a sweeping second hand; the fake ticks off each second. Start watching for this and you will soon be able to tell who is not really SOF material.

A very important point to make here for all of our students: people with piles of money didn't get it by being stupid or throwing their cash away. If you are driving out to the Hamptons, you will drive through many quaint towns where the residents have "beau coop" money. Stop in these shops and you will see that the rich love getting a deal too! As one rich matron was overheard saying, "I love to brag about how much money I saved versus how much money I spent."

**Flaunt Fiscal Tip**: If one does not have the funds to wear the latest and greatest fashions, simply don a classic style and stick to it. A blue blazer and khaki pants work for both men and women. Actually, a blazer will go nicely with jeans, khakis, or slacks. Ladies can never go wrong with black pencil pants and a crisp white shirt! We mean CRISP, students! Again, clean, clean, clean attire should be worn at all times! One can always wear ballet-style flats, readily available at most any retail establishment. We are speaking of the ladies, but we do not judge. We love Tory Burch flats! Do some homework, students, and research Tory's line. Then, you will know what to look for in a cute pair of flats, whether shopping at Target or Talbot's.

**Flaunt Flash News**: The following International Designers are reported to be circling the parking lot at Target (or Targét, as we like to call it): Tucker, Tracy Feith, Paul & Joe, Jonathan Saunders, Termperly of London, Behnaz Sarafpour, Erin Featherstone, Rodarte, Luella Bartley, Tara Jarmon, Thakoon, Libertine, and Jovovich-Hawk! Prices starting at $24.99! Just look at how Missoni went over at Target ... selling out in a number of hours! Crashing their web sites, et all.

Wait! Rumor has it that Karl Lagerfeld is hanging at H & M!! True. No more excuses. You can learn to dress well for less!

****

If you are driving your eco-friendly electric car, or the Mercedes; have on a few good pieces of jewelry; and are carrying a good handbag (not a knock-off Gucci); you have made the statement that you have style. Style is what you are aiming for—not faddish style you see so-called celebrities wearing to get in the latest tabloid magazine, but the kind of look that screams "quiet money."

"What is quiet money?" you ask. You would know this if you had come from old money, and wouldn't be questioning our point. So, students, please note this fine distinction between new and old money: "old" money is the kind of money that has been handed down through generations. It does not have to prove anything. There is a certain reserve and understated elegance to quiet, old money. These people scream, silently, by their very persona and choice of clothes, "I've got it."

Old moneyed people have a way of carrying themselves into a room or restaurant that makes heads turn. A slight aside here: remember, if you see someone like this, do not stare. We repeat, do not stare! You can take in this picture with a few discreet glances and imprint this permanently into your memory. One last thought, and it is very important—check out their shoes. Yes, check out their shoes. Why? Oh, dear students, because no one who has money wears cheap shoes.

It just doesn't happen. It would be like wearing shoes with holes in the soles. We grimace at the very thought. Ghastly!

****

Continuing on, lets now talk about casual wear. Good choices are Banana Republic, Talbot's and Polo or your SOF logo wear. All are totally appropriate for lounging about, doing errands, playing golf or tennis, or for that quick day spa trip. (Note: The classic tennis sweater is making another triumphant return.) When in Palm Beach or the Hamptons don't be without a few Lilly Pulitzer casuals. There is ever so much "old money" style in that look. Remember, you are striving for that "old money, quiet money" look.

Alas, some of you are thinking you need to look frumpy, like the Queen of England, who, we might add, for a lady of a certain age, still looks amazing. Please do have proper respect for royalty and age, students. But we digress … we are not espousing looking dowdy, or like an old dowager!

So, you are still puzzled and don't understand what we are striving for here? Read on, and hopefully you will start to get the picture, because this is the look that will help you fit in anywhere, and we do mean in the places that count!

Old money does not gravitate to the gaudy. We repeat here, do not be gaudy. Don't over-accessorize! Yes, we are screaming at you to make the point! Additionally, old money does not show cleavage, as if preparing to perform at the local strip club. Yes, you read right, and you also know who you are: you wear polyester tank tops or something cut down to your navel. You think that you are oh-so sexy— NOT! If looking like a hooker working the corner is sexy, then you've got it, babe. (We'll get into plastic surgery and sizes in a later lesson.) As Mrs. Braithwaite used to say to Alexandra, "Remember, darling, leave something to the imagination. It is really more alluring. Men like to use their imaginations." Those words of wisdom will always hold true.

On to Grunge: it is dead! Even your jeans should be of the best quality. Look to True Religion, Rock & Republic, 7 for All Mankind, or Hudson Jeans. Say, "Goodbye!" to Old Whatever and be prepared to pay, big-time! Hudson Jeans, for example, go for between $215 and $325. You think that is high? Well, think $995! We kid you not. Hudson Jeans also makes one- of-a-kind, hand-cut, hand-sewn jeans; not totally couture, but close to it. If you hear someone say, "Resurrection," snap to attention. These are one-of-a-kind Hudson's! Also remember that if your jeans don't make you look taller and thinner, you should put them back on the shelf and continue shopping.

**Flaunt Flash News**: Hudson jeans were seen at Costco. Only $110 a pair! Run!

Yes, you can have a hole in your jeans but only if the manufacturer has put it there, and you are under 35. Please, students, do not wear any clothing that is really worn out. It will only scream, "Ugly!" in most cases. If you are a movie star, you can get away with it. Let us remind you—you are not a movie star. Throw away those worn out clothes now! Please, no frayed collars, holes, or tears in your clothing. These are major flaunt failures!

This is a very important SOF rule to follow, and we cannot impress upon you how important this rule is: dress appropriately for your age and body type. How many times have you seen a middle-aged woman who still thinks she is twenty and wears a size four? We're begging you here, ladies, LOOK IN THE MIRROR. You look ridiculous in hip-hugging jeans with muffin tops rolling over the low-cut waist band. Yes, again you know who you are, and some of you younger women are just as guilty! You lean over and have that "beached whale" look in those jeans! Stop kidding yourselves! Unless you are wafer thin, pull down that T-shirt and cover up that baby fat.

FAT, FAT, FAT! It is not pretty, and don't think that it is sexy, either. It reeks of tacky, no taste, and no self respect. Sorry to be so harsh; this hurts us more than it does you. Some of you just need to have that wake-up call, or some Spanks that will smooth out those not-so appealing areas. Next time you are getting ready to pop another chip into your mouth, stop. Think of the Biggest Loser … is that you? Are you losing all of that weight or are you a total Flaunt Failure?

**Note**: We do not condone the anorexic look. That one is ghastly as well as unhealthy!

****

Now, we don't want to forget our young men. Do you really think that anyone wants to see your underwear while your pants are hanging below your "cheeks?" Or even worse, the dreaded COIN SLOT! You've all seen it. Makes you want to run for the nearest exit! Please! This is not an acceptable look for our students!

We don't want you sitting beside us, or even sitting on something the general public has to sit on, if that is how you are wearing your pants. Do we need to paint a picture? Think about it! It is UGLY!! Oh, for the days of a good tight-fitting pair of jeans on a great body! Why would you want to wear baggy pants and show off faded, used underwear? We pray that this look will also go the way of Grunge, and quickly!

SOF men, please STOP whatever you are doing now and go out and buy some great jeans. You fellows only have those cute derrieres for a short period of time! "Derriere?" you say. "What is that?" It is French for your "bottom." Please, students, start using that word instead of slang words like butt, fanny, or bum (to the Brits.) All are terribly gauche. We know fellows, if derriere is too girlie for you, then just avoid referring to your butt! Merci!

Gentlemen, this is very important. Do you work on the East Coast, in the Midwest or on the West Coast? When in NY, do as the New Yorkers do and so on. You can never go wrong with the Wall Street look—single-breasted, dark blue Hickey Freeman suit, spread-collar dress shirt, hand-rolled, linen handkerchief and, definitely, gold cuff links. Top this off with a Brioni or Hermés tie and you are now true SOF material. To finish your look, don't forget that custom made dress shirt (preferably from a British or Italian tailor.) When in London, stop into Turnbull & Asser for truly wonderful men's dress shirts. You may buy off the shelf or have them custom made! Kings have been known to wear their shirts! Move over Prince Charles,—a School of Flaunt devotee just entered the room.

Continuing on … we realize that custom suits have wide appeal, since you can choose your own fabric and details. But, you can purchase off the rack, so to speak, and find something great in the process, too. Prices range from $3,000 for an Issey Miyake, to $3,800 for a Giorgio Armani, up to slightly over $6,000 for a Brioni. Gentlemen, find your look and stick to it! Hopefully, you don't think that pants like M.C. Hammer wore are the height of fashion! Remember, gentlemen can use your PWC, too, and your tailor should be your best friend.

So important—don't forget your choice of a watch! During the day and for business, a gold Rolex President should be worn. For evening wear, get out the Piaget (which will nicely spruce up your Ermenegildo Zegna or Paul Smith suit..) They get our seal of approval.

Ladies, remember that your Rolex Oyster Perpetual or a gold Rolex can take you through the day, as well. Some of you might also prefer a Jaeger LeCoultre Reverso, which is fine. Please take our advice here—and go with a gold Cartier or Piaget, with a little bling we call diamonds, for the evening. The first several watches mentioned are way too business-like for evening wear or, for that matter, fun! We will discuss jewelry and watches in more detail in Lesson Three.

But, we digress and need to return to custom, because this really takes us into another stratosphere of dressing. Remember the letters DQ. What do they stand for? NO, NOT DAIRY QUEEN! Duncan Quinn, men's fashions extraordinaire. DQ offers high-end luxury items for men; from custom made suits (please refer to them as "Bespoke") which are cut from the finest materials ranging from $4,000 to $15,000 depending on variables, to custom shirts, ties and handkerchiefs. If ordering custom shirts, remember there is a 4 shirt minimum,—well worth it!

**Flaunt Flash News**: DQ even has motorcycle helmets! And, so that you can still have that powerful fashion statement even with casual dress, they have a croquet shirt and a polo shirt. We kid you not. What, pray tell, is the difference? We're told a croquet shirt has a crest or skullcap on it which is centered below the buttons, as opposed to being positioned to the side like the Polo shirt. Who knew? Now you do! You may not plead ignorance to your professors at the School of Flaunt now.

Remember, gentlemen, your clothes should always be about fit, color and the correct business or casual look. Always be a SOF man; the one who wears the right clothes to every event. The man that people love to take those furtive looks at. We are smiling at the picture of you now! May we point out movie star George Clooney? He is sauve, debonair and always well dressed. You could do worse than to emulate him. We might add here that he had a terrific role model; his father, Nick Clooney. Having had the pleasure of talking with him, he was always the epitome of a gentleman. He is totally charming and this man knows how to dress! Small towns in Kentucky do turn out some wonderful successes. Even well respected artists. Again, who knew?

Now, if you think after all of this that Dog the Bounty Hunter is a role model for dressing, we at the School of Flaunt throw up our hands in total exasperation. Get thyself to Big Lots! and never darken our path again. Thank you!

****

One last little detail for the well dressed executive or entrepreneur to know. Don't carry a Samsonite brief case. PLEASE! It is so bourgeois, i.e., middle class and humdrum. You should only have a beautiful leather brief case and it should also come with a matching attache. NO, we don't mean a person appointed to an Ambassador's staff, but a small flat rectangular case for carrying documents, etc., when you don't need a brief case. This point applies to both gentlemen and ladies. You can be considered SOF material in the board room or any meeting now. Check out Proenza Shoulder Satchels at Barneys. Lovely.

One final note. Probably at one time or another you may have owned a plaid sports jacket. BURN IT IMMEDIATELY! Subdued madras pants are again acceptable for the Country Club or possibly, at a Polo match. For those of you who have never gone to a Polo match, learn what a chucker is and bring only the best champagne to drink during the match! You can now hang out with "The Donald," but make sure that you are up on business and world affairs, too!

We almost forgot, students. "The eyes don't lie": Check out the following designer sun glasses and puh-leese, do not wear fake! Real feels ever so much better, e.g., Chanel, Gucci, Alain Mikli, Tom Ford, Oliver Peoples and Prada. Framing is everything! Find the right size and style for your face; not just the right name.

**Flaunt Flash News**: Check out custom eyewear designed by Nader Zadi. His designs are available in all types of shapes and sizes, but just what makes them special? All of his frames are produced from 19th & 20th century pieces from eyemakers who are no longer in business. From elaborate filigree, rare and one-of-a-kind materials including spring bridges and mother of pearl nose pads, these 12 and 14 carat little beauties can run you from $750 to $5,000 a pair. Think round, oval, almond, triangular or even hexagonal shapes. Unfortunately, he only has one shop in Manhattan at this time, but maybe, if the School of Flaunt Gods are aligned correctly, he will be opening up boutiques in other cities. We can only hope!

**Flaunt Fiscal Tip**: Ray Ban Sun Glasses are of a modest price and a classic style that will not let you down. Use Ray Ban frames for regular spectacles as well!

****

Last, but not least, are your children. Remember, they are a reflection of you. Start them with handmade baby outfits and smocked dresses. Move on to designer duds but please, no diamond jewelry until they are 21. Rabbit should only be worn until the age of 14 for our SOF young ladies. After that they should only wear fun furs of the sheered variety. Mink should never be worn until after college graduation. No exceptions to that rule! We will add here that if your daughter is having a self esteem issue because of you saying "good job" for the millionth time, and the world now lets her know that it wasn't a good job, then do get her a fun little fur coat to wear. Amazing how that can just spark a new attitude!

We should add that we are not endorsing the wearing of real fur. Let your conscience be your guide on that matter. And, think about how embarrassing it would be for you to have someone from PETA throw something at you or your child when either of you had on that fur coat. Just a thought, students.

But we digress. Most importantly, we need to remind you that children should never look like caricatures of adults. Please, how many Mommies do you see with daughter in tow who could be described by Mom as "my little me?" Perish the thought. Awful! Cutesy matching outfits for Mom and daughter. Ladies, stop. Don't do it. What are you thinking? No matching blouses or dresses. Never! And we do mean never! If your baby girl loves your Ferragamo bag, get her a little one in another color and design. Katie & Tom Cruise's daughter was spied with her little bag. So cute!

Lastly, we know this is a sensitive topic, but remember you are not dressing your daughter for a children's beauty pageant. The rule for age appropriate dressing applies to our children, too. No makeup, no finger nail polish, no baby bikinis. Have we made our point? We can only hope that we have!

****

In closing, we are not suggesting that you spend "willy nilly" here. We want you to be discriminating! Pick those classics that will stay in style for a long time and then accessorize with new trendy items for that updated look. There you are, another classic beauty who is the epitome of SOF! Whew, we know a lot of information! Did you take notes? You better say yes!

Now go out and make us proud!

# Lesson One Quiz

1. What do you do as soon as you enter your favorite store?
    a.  Scream for a salesperson!
    b.  Have your body guard clear the way for you to proceed to your favorite department.
    c.  Having called ahead, the owner or manager is there to personally assist you or, at the very least, your PWC!

ANSWER: C

2. What should give you a headache when shopping?
    a.  Shoes with clear plastic heels
    b.  Anything gold electroplated
    c.  Knock-offs sold out of the trunk of someone's car
    d.  All of the above

ANSWER: D

3. Who are Prada, Burberry and Hermés?
    a.  A local law firm
    b.  Imported wines
    c.  Discriminating stores to frequent for handbags, coats and scarves etc.

ANSWER: C

4. What is a Bon Vivant?
    a.  A great chocolate dessert
    b.  A Famous race horse
    c.  A Rock Star
    d.  A person who indulges in good living

e. Someone we would like you to be

f. D & E

ANSWER: F – (Sorry, students, we didn't use this term before so it is a slight trick question but now you can use it! And hopefully be known as one soon.)

5. Who is Englishman Charles Frederick Worth?
   a. Founding father of haute couture in Paris in 1858
   b. First designer to have designer labels
   c. Started presentations for seasonal collections
   d. Clients came to him not vice versa
   e. All of the above

ANSWER: E – All of the above! We didn't mention his name because this is why you do research! Here is a little story about him. Charles Dickens, as in the writer, students, allegedly reported back that a bearded man with his fingers was allowed to take the exact dimensions of the highest titled women in Paris—robe them, unrobe them, and then make them turn around! Today we call them stylists and PWC's.

6. Describe quiet money? This is not a multiple choice question. If you can't describe "quiet money" go back to the beginning of the lesson and please start again.

7. Name the three best clothing stores in your area in three seconds!

If you could not, you just got an F! Do not proceed to the next lesson. Review the wardrobe in Lesson One thoroughly!

8. How does a SOF student dress?
    a.  Over the top
    b.  Mid-rift on display, showing lots of cleavage
    c.  Wears only clingy, trashy clothes
    d.  Dresses age and body appropriate
    e.  Tries to copy the Pamela Anderson look

ANSWER: D – Did you get the picture?

9. What should you always remember when shopping?

ANSWER: THEY ARE TRYING TO SELL CLOTHES IN THE
DEPARTMENT STORES! THIS MIGHT NOT WORK FOR
YOU! THINK … IS THIS FLATTERING TO MY FIGURE? IF
THE ANSWER IS MAYBE NOT, THEN PUT IT BACK ON THE
HANGER AND WALK AWAY!!

10. Where can you wear a sweatsuit?
    a.  At home when watching television
    b.  At home when you are exercising
    c.  At home when you are gardening
    d.  At home when you have no intentions of answering the door
    e.  At home ONLY!
    f.  All of the above

ANSWER: F – Please don't wear those outside of the home. Maybe
you might consider this if you are popping in and out of the Exercise
Club that you belong to, but remember this; God forbid that you are
in an accident and people see you in that tired, over-washed, bleached
out thing. And then there's that moment when you say, "Oh I need
a carton of milk," so you run into the local market and meet everyone that you haven't seen for the last year! It happens!! Will make an
exception for Juicy Couture.

11. What do Dog the Bounty Hunter, MC Hammer, George Clooney and Nick Clooney have in common?
    a. Probably nothing
    b. Nothing
    c. Absolutely nothing
    d. All of the above

ANSWER: D – From the School of Flaunt's vantage point, we think this group is an unlikely foursome!

12. Trick Question: Who designed Kate Middleton's wedding dress when she wed Prince William in Westminster Abbey?
    a. Karl Lagerfeld
    b. Stella McCartney
    c. Sarah Burton
    d. Georgio Armani

ANSWER: C – Sarah Burton for Alexander McQueen and it was kept totally secret until the ceremony!

## LESSON TWO:
## Salons and Spas … Ah the Good Life!

"Fresh, Sassy, Edgy and Totally Chic"

IT IS NOW time to indulge yourself in those fantasies and make them a reality with a new you! If you haven't heretofore been pampered, GET READY!! In every major city, you can luxuriate at the best spa bastions, and we are not talking about a sweat lodge, here! Get a facial, massage, pedicure, manicure and salt rub now! After a hectic entrepreneur's day, it should be "Red Door" time. What is the Red Door? A slice of pure heaven, otherwise known as an Elizabeth Arden Spa!

Try the newest salt glow rubs, mud wraps, hot stone, lavender, chocolate, Swedish and sport massages at your favorite Five Star Resort or Hotel! Don't forget all great spas have waxing, make-up, massage, manicures and pedicures. Think, Caviar Pedies anyone?

**Flaunt Flash News**: For hair removal you may consider threading or sugaring, also called khite. Threading is an ancient method that was practiced in Egypt and India. A cotton thread is pulled along unwanted hair in a twisting motion; think of a lasso that simply lifts the hair right out of the follicle. This technique is so fast that a skilled practitioner can give you amazing eyebrows in 2 minutes and, better yet, no chemicals are applied to the skin. This method of hair removal is only done for the face, though. So, you are saying, what can we do for the rest of the body? Try sugaring! This is also an ancient middle eastern practice that uses an all natural paste or gel. Results can last up to six weeks and it is said to be less painful than waxing. We think that Cleopatra knew these tricks! Wish she was here so we could get the details. After all, she was probably one of the first women who really knew how to be "flaunt fabulous."

Students, do you really think that those celebs look that great with only the help of Mother Nature? Puh-leese, it doesn't happen. Remember, we said waxing, threading or sugaring. You ask, where? Frankly, any place that has hair will do! Think back, chest, underarms, chin, full face and eyebrows. The dreaded Bikini line can be taken care of with a Brazilian wax. Throw in eyelash extensions or eyelash and eyebrow tints and some acrylic nails for your fingers, and you will now look like you could be in the movies, too. Small aside here: we prefer natural nails over acrylic. If you can't grow your nails then you can go fake but please, NO TALONS. And don't have cutesy, little art work drawn on them, either. We shudder at that look, totally non-SOF!

Here are a few SOF Spa Flaunt Favorites:

## Body Treatments
### Dead Sea Mud Wrap
Using an ancient mud that re-mineralizes, exfoliates and detoxifies the body, leaving you revitalized, refined and rejuvenated.

### Mineral Salt Glow
Using salt from Salt Island, the body is completely exfoliated. This invigorating treatment is finished with a moisturizing massage.

### Neem Leaf Body Wrap
Handpicked Neem leaves have therapeutic properties. They are made into a mask that is placed on the body, detoxifying, invigorating, and reducing blemishes, leaving the skin wonderfully clear and silky smooth.

**Aloe Body Wrap**

This uses locally grown aloe combined with essential oils and moisturizers which soothe, restore, and rehydrate sunburned skin.

<u>**Massages**</u>

**Ultimate Swedish**

90 minutes of a combination of techniques to give you the perfect massage and total relaxation.

**Hot Stone Therapy**

Warmed basalt stones combined with massage melt away tension and re-balance your body.

**La Stone Massage**

A ceremony that begins with a chakra opening and placement of chakra stones followed by a full body massage using deep moist heated Basalt stones and ending with a complete chakra closing.

**Indian Massage**

With this full body, face and scalp massage, you will enjoy this Traditional invigorating treatment.

**Thai Massage**

A combination of stretching, massage, acupressure, etc., aligns the energy channels of the body.

**Couples Massage**

If you cannot stand to be apart, enjoy an hour of relaxation together in the massage room, beach or anywhere for two.

<u>**Facial Treatments**</u>

**Deep Cleansing Facial**

Cleansing, toning, exfoliation, mask and a wonderfully relaxing moisturizing massage.

**Aloe Facial**
Local Aloe combined with essential oils and hydrating moisturizers sooths, restores and re-hydrates sun dried skin.

**The MAN made Facial**
A nourishing facial formulated for men. Includes cleansing, hot towels exfoliation and skin-smoothing mask to make the face look and feel younger.

## Spa Retreats & Experiences
**Traveler's Jet Lag Relief**
Relaxing Aroma Massage
Deep Cleansing Facial

**The Aromatherapy Experience**
Aroma Salt Glow
Relaxing Aroma Massage
Aroma Facial

Enjoy the spa and tip generously! You will always be welcomed back!

**Flaunt Fiscal Tip**: Most massage schools give free or very inexpensive spa treatments. Check these out, students. We at the School of Flaunt must draw the line at certain "Massage Parlors"—a big SOF NO-NO to that one!

****

Now each of us only has so much time, and going to a spa is time consuming. How can you relax and improve your mood and spirit? Well, dear students, fragrance is now thought to influence just that. Think aromatherapy in your beauty products. Grapefruit, orange, lemon, and lime seem to bring out a happy mood. Lavender can be used for relaxation and roses are known as a sedative. Look for those scented bath and body products to use in your shower or bath. Light a candle at night that has a wonderful scent and turn on the sound machine of the ocean rolling into the beach. We can already feel the stress leaving you now.

Lastly, during the day, ladies, you can try a special fragrance. Note: you do not want to be "splashing" it on. Remember those women in the office or on a plane that just have to keep applying their favorite scent. Everyone is dying around them! A light spritz will do nicely, or a simple dab on your wrist a few times a day. Capisce?

Here are a few of our favorite perfumes. They not only smell lovely but their bottles will look outstanding on your dressing table.

Van Cleef & Arpels, Oriens $150, 100 milliliters. A beautiful ornate bottle crowned with a multicolored jewel-cut stopper inspired by a tourmaline and diamond ring. As only a French jeweler could design this bottle it is complemented with silver leaves. Think fruity berry, cherry floral, with a hint of patchouli after it dries. Yum! Should we wear it or make a cocktail out of it?

Balenciaga Paris, $95, 1.7 ounces. A stunning bottle finished off with a unique stopper that speaks French fashion-house chic. Violet aromas will delight your senses as if you were in a mossy woods. Picture yourself on a cashmere throw, relaxing under a large maple with dappled sunlight coming through it. Add a glass of French champagne and it is a perfect School of Flaunt afternoon.

Van Cleef & Arpels, Feerie, $250, 1.01 oz. This unique cabochon bottle of Sapphire blue with a beautiful little fairy sitting on a delicate twig is full of whimsy and will add a wonderful touch to your dressing table. Think woody violet, tonka bean, and rich vanilla. Remember, you can start the little ones out with their own bottle of Feerie too. It would be so cute on their dresser!

Chanel Chance eau Tendre, $65, 1.7 ounces. Again, a stunning bottle with a discreet Chanel printed on the front. For when you want to be in a flirty young outfit or after finishing a game of tennis. Think grass and clover with an overtone of grapefruit. Perfect for those grass court tennis matches, don't you agree? Everyone needs a touch of Chanel; then put on some of their divine lipstick and you are good to go!

Joy Baccarat Pure Parfum. A simple must have for any SOF devotee. Price is no object for this 50 limited edition perfume. From Jean Patou Joy and their flower fields in Grasse over a two week period they collect 10,600 flowers required for each bottle. Bulgarian rose, ylang-ylang, tuberose and grasse jasmine combine to take you to SOF Heaven. Remember, students, only a small dab. There can be too much of a good thing!

So many perfumes to explore. Please enjoy the journey and start a collection of beautiful bottles today.

**\*\*\*\***

School of Flaunt students, you need to really get down to business now. Here are your steps for a true SOF makeover.

First, seek a great hair stylist and develop a real relationship. Spare no expense and remember your crowning glory morning, noon and night! A pretty bob or layered mane will take you anywhere. Or, think Oprah when she goes curly and sassy. We love that look on her!

If you have fine hair and decide to use extensions, think twice here, students. We have seen some really horrid heads that have extensions. If you aren't prepared to spend the big bucks and properly take care of them, please don't go that route. Bottom line, students; if you don't have hair like Penelope Cruz, stay away from the long locks. You'll only end up looking like you have straggly hair. Not a good look on anyone! Stay with that short and sassy, classic version of a Vidal Sassoon that came into vogue in the 60s and is still here with variations. Your hairdresser will understand what we are talking about.

Ladies, we don't intend to be mean but if you are 45 plus, think about cutting that long hair. Picture a woman in her 50s or 60s, slight or major greying, hair down past her shoulders. It can only be described as UGGGLY! You know what we mean. We've all seen them in the local market and wanted to run at them with scissors in hand, jump them like a professional wrestler and start hacking off those tresses. Or there is the woman who still thinks she looks chic with those tight little curls all over her head that are laquered with a gallon of hair spray so they can't move! Puh-leese ... we nick-named her Helmet Head! Lastly, there is the frizzy look. Ever hear of a flat iron? These women are just lazy. We can hear them exclaiming, "Oh, I just love this hair style. All I have to do is get up in the morning and wash my hair and let it dry naturally." Natural is not good for you! Please, will someone get us some tissues? We don't know whether to cry or laugh at you.

As for you men, we are not letting you off, either. Think "pony tail" on someone who is half bald. We've all seen them and thought, "You look ridiculous." That is when you'll want those scissors again; to silently sneak up on them and whack it off! Let's face it guys, if you aren't in the entertainment industry or have a PhD, you can't pull off being eccentric. Just put yourself in the hands of a stylist, too. We promise they will take years off of your age and get the ladies to start looking again. A small aside: Brett Michaels can pull off any pony tail, but we still want to know what is under that bandana. Then there is Hulk Hogan. We can only picture what is under his bandana but maybe, we don't want to!

A true story: Do any of you remember the late movie actress, Mae West? Queen of the phrase, "Come up and see me sometime." Well when she was approximately in her 70s, she tottered onto the plane along with her manager and entourage. Poor Mae, if she only knew that when she was seated, or for that matter standing, since she was quite short, that anyone could look down on the top of her head. There was the nasty tale of bad extensions for all to see. Thinning hair, pink scalp and loose extensions. So sad! Please, students, we don't want this for any of you. One last point: why do some women think it unnecessary to take a mirror and look at the back of their heads? Enough said, because we have reached our level of frustration on this topic!

Hopefully we do not need not to remind you that your hair should always be fastidious and clean. And never color at home. We repeat here, NEVER! Picture that woman with dark brown hair that has turned slightly red, with her roots showing a third color. We've all seen this and flinched as they walked by. And then there are the men who decide that they don't want that little touch of grey and all of sudden show up at the work place with dyed black hair and, even worse, a dyed black mustache. What are you thinking, students? You can look absolutely ghastly with at-home products and amateur treatments!

Continuing on, while we are are quite sure that most of you at one time or another have been sitting in your stylist's chair, only to be able to overhear the conversation of another stylist with their client. The client has brought in a picture of their favorite hair style to show the stylist. The conversation seems to go on ad nauseam about how much the client loves this hair style. You are looking at them from the corner of your eye, thinking "Please, who are you kidding? You are never going to look good in that cut." Now, most stylists will be honest with you about the texture of your hair, the cut and color but you can be in the hands of a pure amateur who is only interested in their pay check. How do you avoid this terrible fate? It is expensive, but you need to go to one of the top salons in a major city.

Now, here is the drill students: you will meet with the stylist. They will conduct an interview with you about what hair cut will be most flattering for your facial contour. They will not discuss what your favorite celeb is doing! Your stylist will then give you to the colorist, where he or she will explain exactly how they want you colored down to the highlights, of course. Remember, the colorist is an expert, too. Don't argue with these professionals. That is why you are paying the big bucks; for their expertise, not your fantasies. Have we made ourselves perfectly clear? Shake your head yes, thank you.

Continuing on. While you are being colored (and this is the yummy part) someone will come in and give you a neck and shoulder massage, plus your favorite beverage. Enjoy. You are paying dearly for this pampering!

Your high paid stylist will glide in and out of the room occasionally to check your color and, if need be, recommend any additional highlighting to the colorist. Then your "Guru" of style will return for your cut! Most likely they will not blow your hair dry but an assistant will. The stylist will give your new look the proper finishing touches with a flick of their magic fingers, lightly apply some hair spray and suggest new hair products to keep your color looking fresh. Have your Black Amex card ready, for this experience will probably range in the price of $250 to $800 depending on the city but it is worth every penny. Remember anyone who comes NEAR you in that salon should receive a tip! Take lots of cash! Lastly, not only will you look like a million dollars but your new SOF look will pay dividends in the future.

A word of advice: if you leave a salon with the "hump" look on the top and back of your head, i.e., a ratted mass of hair resembling a Camel's hump, you do not have a Guru of style let alone a stylist. Walk away and never come back! In fact, take out your jogging shoes and run away as fast as you can from that salon. Remember we are trying to get you out of the 1900s—the days of the 60s, 70s, 80s and 90s. Work with us here, students! Think of the Jersey Shore TV program. This is what you definitely don't want! No Snookie look! Sorry darling! Where is our bowl of milk? Meow …

A small aside: Have you been thinking of having some plastic surgery? Try a new hair cut first. Bangs are the new Botox! You might be surprised but bangs can take off years. And remember both extremes of long, straggly hair or too short can add years to your face. Do you really enjoy looking dowdy or 10-20 years older than you really are? A trained hair stylist at the top salons knows all the tricks of the trade. Why do you think that the Hollywood types pay these people so much money for just a color and cut? It isn't only for name dropping! Whether you are young or old, SOF devotees, heed this advice—sassy and bouncy is not only for children's hair!

**Flaunt Flash News**: Brazilian Blow Outs, which are a hot new trend for those of you who were not blessed with straight hair, are now being questioned. HORRORS! What is a woman to do that only wants to stop her hair from being unmanageable or totally frizz free? It looks like some of these products have an unacceptably high level of formaldehyde in them. Yes, you and your stylist are breathing in toxins. Not good!

We have also learned that since the customer only has to have this treatment every twelve weeks, whereas the stylist is doing many of these a day, that the real harm might only be to the stylists. So, Students of Flaunt, we can only advise you to be very careful. We know the allure of having the option to do curly, wavy or a straight blow dry for some of you is just too much to not try. Plus, we have seen the results and they are outstanding, as well they should be for $300 to $400!

Dear students, if you want a Brazilian Blow Out, you have been forewarned. As always, we suggest that you do your homework. And last, if you decide this is a must do, then tell your stylist that you don't want to pay $300; try to get a discount. We do so love those! Remember, Flaunt Fiscal! Just a thought, students. That $100 you are saving can pay for your pedicure, manicure and tip. HAPPY HAIR DAYS at the salon!

**Note**: Please no hair flipping, ladies. You are not trying out for the Dallas Cowboys' Cheerleading Squad. Nor are you a member of the Kardashian family. A very tiresome habit for those of us who have to watch you!

**Flaunt Find**: Gossip, students: Sally Hershberger, a celebrity in her own right, is known for cutting Meg Ryan's hair. She has salons in West Hollywood and NYC. Hair cuts can run from a mere $150 to $800. Michael Canale has his own salons in Beverly Hills and Malibu. His clients are even from NYC and Washington, D.C., so be prepared to wait for an appointment with him. We understand that Jennifer Aniston has gotten her hair colored and highlighted by Michael.

Don't forget Frederic Fekkai Salons, which have five locations, but this is the very best! Plan on going to St. Barts, French West Indies, and vacation at the Hotel Guanahani, which is home to one of Frederic's salons! An appointment with Frederic is almost impossible but do try, students. So much flaunt in that appointment!

****

Now, continuing with steps for your makeover. Think Hoda Kotb and Kathie Lee going "all natural" on one of their shows. Yes, they really did! Ladies, that was not a good thing! But the good news is, in that morning "shock picture," it proves everyone looks better with makeup. Whoops … having said that we really do love Hoda and Kathie Lee!

May we ask you, do you think SOF would approve of black nails and pounds of black eyeliner? We hope that your answer was not yes. If so read on.

When you look in the mirror, is Lady Gaga (the ultimate in shock value, who makes us feel like someone just used a taser on us) or Adam Lambert staring back at you? They are all about the theatrics, students. You are NOT! Last time we looked you were not a rock star or a celeb trying to make sure you got into *People* magazine or booked in Las Vegas. Makeup is supposed to enhance your looks—not send small children screaming for their Mothers!

SOF devotees, we are begging you here (yes, you may picture us begging) please have a professional do your makeup and update often. Most top of the line salons will do your makeup after you get that new hairdo. Take advantage of the time and spend the entire day, if possible. Have your hair, make up, pedicure and manicure all done. A day of pure SOF hedonistic pleasures. Love, love, love that! And guess what? You can walk out looking like a movie star, not a rock star. Please consult Lesson Six on Attitude to pull together the new you!

You say you're afraid of changing your look? Don't be afraid. Please have no fear. These makeup artists will teach you how to properly apply everything. They will show you the right brushes to use, how to use them and how to combine colors. Again they are so useful when it comes to age appropriate makeup. These "flaunt artistas" of the makeup brush can give you that flawless skin and take years off of the tired entrepreneur. They will give you a new, updated, fresh and flawless look. Now, aren't you "Flaunt" fabulous! Our School of Flaunt devotees are ready for the "red carpet" now!

We must add a small note here: Mothers of daughters who are in their first stages of doing their own makeup should be taken to a "flaunt artista," too. This would make a wonderful Mother-Daughter day out together, but, what is more important, you are starting her out properly on how to apply her makeup. Recently, we, at the School of Flaunt, were at our salon of choice and took note of two young women. Why are we bringing this up? Because they looked like their makeup was put on with a spatula. Ladies, you are not a cake! You don't need piles of makeup; just as a cake doesn't need to be over-iced! Take your daughters with you for makeup lessons and they will thank you. Who knows, they might end up being the next top model. Seven figure salaries aren't all that bad, are they?

One last thought. Please, ladies, when you are at home, take the time to buff your heels. There is nothing more distasteful than seeing crusty, scaly, peeling heels, peering out from underneath those Christian Louboutin sling back heels that you just spent the big bucks for. Don't you think it ruins the picture? You may as well go to Target and buy a pair of rubber flip-flops! A small note here: Those rubber flip-flops, if purchased in Palm Desert, Boca or Naples, will probably have some bling on them, and you may wear them to the beach or around your pool. Rubber should know its place.

We probably should have mentioned this under wardrobe but, while most flip-flops are usually cheap and made out of plastic, guess what? If you really want to flaunt those freshly pedicured toes poolside, look at Crystalishious. Their flip-flops are covered in crystals and will stand out in a crowd. Not your usual rubber! But for total fabulous "Flaunt," try H. Stern jeweler, who sold a pair of flip-flops in 2004 for $17,000. Yes, you read right! They were covered in gold feathers and accented with diamonds. So much for crystals. We understand this was the only pair made; now they are probably a collector's item or maybe just thrown into the back of someone's closet? Who knows? Last, for that maximum, comfy feel, try crocodile flip-flops. They will only run you around $400. Seems like a veritable bargain in comparison.

****

Now, you might think this is only for women—listen up SOF men. You are entitled to look and feel you best too! Top salons know this and cater to our SOF men as well.

Remember men, ladies like to see a well-groomed man. Who wants to look at chipped nails and dried out cuticles? If she doesn't want them, why should you? And, if you like a little massage while getting your hair cut and styled, what's wrong with that? Nothing! Go for it! You deserve the best, too.

Here is a little **Flaunt Fiscal Tip** for our SOF students. Have you had a paraffin hand treatment at your favorite salon? You can do the same at home for pennies. All you need is a paraffin therapy bath (which you can buy at most beauty supply outlet), some plastic wrap, hand lotion and a large towel. It is nice to do this while relaxing and watching TV, because you can't move or use your hands while you are giving yourself a treatment. To do this, you will do one hand at a time. Mist your hand lightly with water, use your favorite hand lotion, then dip your hand, with the fingers spread, into the paraffin. Dip your hand a second time. Immediately wrap your hand in plastic wrap or plastic gloves, which you can purchase at any beauty salon, to lock in the heat. Remember to keep your fingers spread slightly, so as not to crack the paraffin. Wrap you hand in a thick terry towel, sit down and relax, keeping your hand warm in the towel. After 15 to 30 minutes, remove the towel and use the plastic wrap or glove to gently remove the paraffin and lotion. Then massage your hand and cuticles with any remaining lotion. Your hand will feel like a baby's bottom. Repeat this procedure for the second hand. Viola! No more crocodile skin. Do this at least once a week—winter or summer. (Please consult Lesson Fourteen for more information about the proper care of the hands.)

Speaking of crocodile skin; ladies, we hope it isn't too late to save your face, neck and decolletage area. Here is another suggestion to help with those wrinkles and dry skin. This recipe comes directly from one of the "Grand Dames of beauty" whose skin still looks wonderful. We vouch for this fact because we have seen the "proof in the pudding," so to speak. We can't guarantee that this will work for you, this is what she has done for years.

**Flaunt Fiscal Tip**: ALWAYS USE SUNSCREEN. NO EXCEPTIONS. REMEMBER, THERE IS SUCH A THING AS SUNLESS TANNING NOW! AGAIN—SAY NO TO THE JERSEY SHORE LOOK.

Here is the Grand Dame's secret for having lovely skin:

**Step One**: **Daily**
1. Never use soap on your face. Cleanse, first, with Cetaphil cleanser.
2. Gently rub your face, neck and chest with Olay Deep Hydration Regenerating Cream. We are not recommending products here. We are merely telling you what she does.
3. Do not rinse.

**Step Two**: **Once a Week**
1. After cleansing with the Cetaphil, dab "Milk of Magnesia" over the same area. Leave on for at least 5 minutes then rinse off. If you don't have "Milk of Magnesia," use avocado. Use the part that is next to the skin, mash it into a smooth paste and apply it to the face.
2. Gently rub Olay Deep Hydration Regenerating Cream on your entire face, neck and chest.
3. Do not rinse
4. Leave on for 5 minutes, then rinse.
5. Use the Olay Cream as described in Step One.

The last tip she gave us was to use egg whites that you have beaten slightly. Dab the beaten egg whites on your face and leave them on for 5 minutes. Then, gently rinse off with warm water. Voila! You have an instant face lift! She does this whenever she feels she needs a lift. It's cheaper than surgery! For those of you who live in a dry part of the country, use a humidifier in your room at night. (Please consult Lesson 14 on Plastic Surgery, if need be.)

But, we have digressed and now need to make one final remark about makeup; between trips to your stylist you might like to make an appointment at one of our favorite makeup spots: the Chanel Boutique!

The talented artists there are worth the wait and the money. Why do you think the French look so good?

Remember, we told you that a SOF devotee has to think quickly on their feet. Quick, who is Bobbie Brown? What are Bare Essentials? Don't know? Go immediately to the makeup counter at Neiman Marcus for a consult. If your preference is leaning more towards drug store products, just remember that you should always take the advice of the real makeup professionals at the top salons. They're paid big bucks by the rich and famous for advice on how to apply makeup. You paid them to apply your makeup and teach you how to do the same. Now, don't forget their techniques with your products of choice and you can't go wrong.

****

Now, at this point in Lesson Two, we want you to go to the mirror and take a critical look at yourself. Mirror, mirror on the wall, who's the fairest of them all? What do you see? Fess up. Is it dark blue eye shadow, ratted hair from the last century and talon-like finger nails? Could it be over-processed hair with absolutely no style or pizazz and tons of black eyeliner? Is it the spatula look for makeup application that we spoke about earlier or the "no makeup" look staring back at you? The mirror does not lie. You definitely are in need of a SOF salon! Go to the phone immediately and make an appointment for a complete make-over. If it requires going to a major city, so be it! Get out your smart phone and make those airline and hotel reservations post haste, or, get in your car and start driving. And, last but not least, remember this is going to be so much fun! Maybe even think girl's weekend! Woo-hoo!!

****

**Your Body is Now a Temple.**

A few extra pounds? Shed them immediately at a chic spa destination. Go for at least a week; bring only what the spa recommends in the way of food-stuff and clothing (usually none of the former and few of the latter). Good spas outfit you in their uniforms. For travel issues head to Nike Town for some cute duds! Don't buy too many—you may be a size smaller soon! Find a health club as soon as you return from this "Boot Camp."

Here are a few helpful hints on choosing your local place of exercise:
1. Who's a Member? This can be beneficial for business, as well as social connections.
2. Location? Only the "Best Part of Town" will do!
3. Private? Preferably. Trendy? Never!

Other details to look for:
A completely current line of exercise equipment, cushioned and banked running tracks, swimming pools (plural), clay and hard courts for tennis, squash courts and steam and sauna rooms; plus multiple massage rooms with a great masseuse! Tai Chi, Hot Yoga, Gentle Yoga, Hatha Yoga, Spin Classes, Kettle Bells, Zumba Dance and Pilates (all levels) are a must! Boot camps, for those in better shape or the truly serious fitness fanatic, are wonderful!

Here's another School of Flaunt tidbit: We know that in today's life all of you are busy and over-worked. Please look into learning Reiki. What did we say? Reiki. It is a Japanese technique for stress reduction and relaxation that also promotes healing. You will now find in some hospitals that they have Reiki masters who will go from room to room and lay on hands if the patient would like. It is simply based on the idea that an unseen life force flows through us. If your life force is low, you are more apt to get sick; if it is high, you are more likely to be happy and healthy. Reiki is not a religion. You may pray, meditate or put yourself in a place where your mind is totally relaxed (such as on a beach or star gazing) while you receive Reiki healing. Whether you learn to meditate, do yoga or receive Reiki, any or all of them may be beneficial. Now breath in slowly and exhale slowly … relax.

But now lets get back to the secrets of a great club: look for a generous quantity of "rolled" towels, (iced or warmed), bottled water at each machine, pitchers of orange, lemon, lime water for additional hydration, which all indicate that the club is well managed and maintained. Second, do not join any club without a carpeted locker room and separate facilities for those less than 18 years of age. Lastly, look for a good healthy restaurant and bar. Need we explain why? SOF does give their blessing to fitness!

**** 

Now we hate to bring up a delicate topic, but we feel that it is necessary because we know that there might be a number of you that need to lose more than a few pounds, plus tone those abs. Here is the secret. You can't do it yourself. Get a personal trainer. Think someone like *Biggest Loser* trainers, Bob Harper or Jillian Michaels. So important, students. We can not accentuate this enough. You need an expert. Sure, those machines on TV look great and those celebs that are using them look wonderful, you bet. Will that happen to you if you use those machines? Maybeeee. But just think if you had a personal trainer who was showing you how to make the most of those machines. Think if you had to show up two days a week, weigh in and talk with your trainer what would probably happen? Most likely those pounds would start to disappear? How do you think that Madonna has the body of a twenty year old? Working out at home on her Nordic Track? Right! Let's get real here, students; she has a fantastic personal trainer who is being paid big bucks to keep her in those "Material Girl" clothes. Just another little thought, don't forget, anything by Gwyneth Paltrow's trainer, Tracy Anderson, who is well worth noting. She is a SOF Fitness Genuis! Pay close attention to Tracy, students!

**Note**: The obesity rate in the U.S.A. still keeps going up. Only you can help yourself! We want all of our School of Flaunt students to have long, healthy and productive lives. "Today is the first day of the rest of your life."

Continuing with fitness, this might surprise you, students, but we know of certain well-heeled people who even have their trainers come with them to their second homes, when they are going for an extended period of time. You shake your head in amazement here. We do not jest when it comes to your health and again, that SOF image where nothing should be left undone. Now start shaping up, toning and bronzing. And by bronzing we are suggesting products, never a tanning bed, e.g., think cancer and dry skin. Heaven forbid! REMEMBER: IT IS ALL ABOUT IMAGE. Now get to work. We want people to watch you enter the room! (Please consult Lesson 6 for more information on SOF Attitude and Manners.)

For a true SOF experience we highly recommend the following Spa Establishments:

**Any Spa at a Four Seasons Hotel**
> www.fourseasons.com

**Any Spa at a Peninsula Hotel**
> www.peninsulahotels.com

**Grand Wailea in Maui, Hawaii**
> www.grandwailea.com

**Canyon Ranch Spas in Tucson, AZ, The Berkshires, Lenox, MA and Las Vegas, NV**
> www.canyonranch.com

**The Golden Door, world renowned in CA**
> www.goldendoor.com

**Miraval Spa in AZ**
> www.miravalresort.com

**The Sanctuary in South Carolina**
> www.thesanctuary.com

# Lesson Two Quiz

1. SOF devotees would never:
    a.  Wear black eye shadow and nail polish
    b.  Color at home
    c.  Dye one's hair to match a pro football team
    d.  Sneak wine into The Golden Door
    e.  a,b,c

ANSWER: E – We confess, we are human.

2. What is Neem?
    a.  A line of men's swim wear
    b.  A Bar in Houston
    c.  Great exercise equipment
    d.  Leaves with cleansing properties for use in facials and wraps
    e.  Jay Leno's masseuse

ANSWER: D

3. What do you find behind the Red Door?
    a.  An Episcopal Church
    b.  A Day Care Center
    c.  Elizabeth Arden
    d.  A true SOF experience
    e.  A & B
    f.  C & D

ANSWER: F

4. Quick! Name Five of the Top Ten Spas in the US?

You couldn't do that? Well you flunked this Lesson. Start at the beginning, underline fine points and memorize! How do you ever think you will be able to hold a conversation around the pool area of any fine home, resort or spa if you can't drop a few names!

5. What is Nautilus?
    a. A boat marina in Marina Del Rey, CA
    b. A line of men's swim wear
    c. A bar in Houston
    d. Great exercise equipment

ANSWER: D – If you couldn't answer this one correctly you certainly have been living under a rock for a long time! Get thyself into the Fitness Club now! Finding a personal trainer should go to the top of your list of things to do today.

6. Which Fashion Designer has created the #1 award winning makeup foundation?
    a. Betsey Johnson
    b. Ralph Lauren
    c. Vera Wang
    d. Georgio Armani

ANSWER: D – This takes research, students, you are never, ever finished with research!

7. Name five fragrances, in thirty seconds, that will help improve your mood.

You couldn't do this? Why do you think you are so stressed out? Go visit a bath shop immediately!

(This page intentionally left blank)

## LESSON THREE:
## Jewels and Furs … The Bling of Flaunt

RULE OF THUMB to follow with Bling: Jewels will never lose their luster and one can never have too many! Some might say wear enough to choke a horse but then, we at SOF think that is going too far!

Now let's get down to the basics: Jewels are extremely personal because of color, but trust us, dripping in them is where you want to be! Diamonds are still anyone's best friend and your jeweler should be at the top of your list for friendships. They can take those family heirlooms and modernize them, if you like. Personally, SOF thinks that heirlooms should be left alone but if they are just too staid or conservative for you please reset into something that suits your personal taste. Emeralds, rubies, any colored stone can be a staple in your jewelry safe. A touch of 18K gold is fun but platinum is preferred.

**Flaunt Flash News**: The first 2010 auction by Sotheby's Australia of a rare red diamond was a FLAUNT FLOP. Sad, but true. They had expected the platinum ring which held an 82 point purple-red diamond, set between two blue diamonds and surrounded by a cluster of white diamonds would fetch between $700,000 to $1,000,000. Bids topped out at $490,000. Rumor has it that there were collectors waiting on the side to make quiet offers for between $800,000 and $900,000. Be on the lookout for that ring at parties.

But, getting back to dressing with your jewels, SOF personally loves a strand of Mikimoto pearls which will never go wrong with that simple black dress. Pearls are our favorite: multi-strands, different types and colors mixed together can make a statement. Remember, students, if you are going multi-strand, please dress simply. The pearls should be the center of attention here. And only simple earrings—pearl or diamond studs or gold loops if you are wearing multi-strands. If you want to make a statement with pearl earrings then go big and forget the strands. Pearl bracelets are always nice but please remember never mix them with any other bracelets—why? Oh, please do we have to explain everything? Because you can scratch your pearls. Remember that advice!

If there is ever a question in your mind, that a stone is too large or pretentious, we suggest this rule of thumb: It is only too big if you have to put your arm in a sling to hold up your hand! Whether you prefer round brilliant, princess cut, pear shape, radiant cut, emerald, cushion or marquis cut, make sure that you know the difference. It is not necessary to compliment someone on the cut of their ring but you never can tell when you might need that tidbit of information for a conversation.

As for you men, never wear a pinkie ring! Think 18 carat gold with an American five dollar piece or a Krugerrand set in it for a nice ring on you third digit. Then there is always your class ring from where you graduated and if you were in a fraternity have those letters engraved on the stone. You'd be surprised at how many doors that might open up for you. (Please consult Lesson Nine for more information on that topic.) We prefer our men to be rather conservative with their jewelry. If you still think that wearing gold chains and leaving your shirt unbuttoned is "au courant" you really need to go back to our first lesson on wardrobe. We do have a migraine coming on just thinking about that look from the 70s. Saturday Night Fever with the old John Travolta look is so over! Polyester pants with bell bottom legs. Sorry students for rambling but PLEASE, SOF GODS, do not let that look ever come back!

But we have digressed and here is another important topic, your brooches! Remember they can become timeless treasures! Add them to complete a look never to over play. Think about pinning a brooch on a plain black silk dress or an evening bag. Hat a little dull? Then dress it up with a lovely pin! Put a brooch on your coat and then there is a gorgeous cashmere shawl that one would look stunning on! Never let these pieces just sit in your jewelry vault. They could be in some cases "family heirlooms and treasures." No excuses, you should be showing them off. We hear you saying to yourself, "I just don't care for them this way." Then consult with your jeweler and have them made into a beautiful piece to clip onto that strand of pearls or gold chain. Where there is a will there is always a way. Make your deceased relatives proud!

**Flaunt Flash News**: Actress Cary Mulligan had a crystal brooch at the waist of her Lanvin dress, which she wore at a red carpet event. Trés chic and completed the look!

Speaking of timeless treasures, renowned King of Bling on Madison Avenue in New York city is Fred Leighton, an expert, on timeless treasures. Believe it or not we heard that he started in the 60s in Greenwich Village peddling Mexican dresses, shoes and gauche used trinkets. Ghastly, we know, but everyone has to start somewhere. So he moved to the Upper East Side and opened a shop selling "estate jewelry." What is estate jewelry? Anything that is less than one hundred years old. After that it is considered an antique which is another subject. But he was clever and we hope that you would be, too. He found his niche and the "rich and famous" made him rich and famous, too. Baubles with stories are always sought after and we do stress always!

Mr. Leighton being the sharp businessman that he is, also started a personal collection consisting of jewelry formerly owned by American and European notables, such as Princess Mathilde Bonaparte, Mrs. Cornelius Vanderbuilt and the Duchess of Windsor. Movie stars' jewels such as Lana Turner and Brigitte Bardot also were claimed in his private treasure trove. We can only fathom how much these beauties will eventually be worth because pieces like this will always increase in value, students. But be forewarned, we want you to know that if there is no story or famous person associated with that stunning piece of jewelry, then the normal rule of thumb is that the market value for any jewelry is only one third of its original price. Sad but true, so we do not recommend buying most jewelry for investment. Please shop carefully and know that once you bought it you will have it forever, or at the very minimum you will have it reset for another look.

Speaking of upper-end jewelers, memorize this name: Joel Arthur Rosenthal or remember the initials J.A.R. Who is he? Born in the Bronx and now a legend on the Place Vendome (Paris, students) he is a reclusive, EXCLUSIVE, Paris designer who only makes one-of-a-kind jewels for appointment-only clients. He usually designs between 70 to 80 pieces a year! You say, " I've been to Paris and never saw his shop?" You silly fool of course you never saw it! He doesn't have a display window, advertise or even have hours. He doesn't need to! You have to make an appointment and you better know someone that he knows or you'll never get a return call back.

Remember this, JAR's pavé designs are fabulous and his "thread" rings which are minute diamonds set in gold and platinum wires look as if they are threaded around one's finger. He even has had the unmitigated audacity to mount diamonds upside down. Yes, the V-shaped base is on the top. Amazing work! Even if you can't remotely afford him you simply must know what JAR stands for. His works rarely come on auction but you can recoup what you paid for them and usually more. A little tidbit here, if you happen to meet Barbara Walters at an evening event she might just have on one of his pieces. This is a SOF moment, ladies. An opportune time to compliment her but don't be so gauche as to ask if she is wearing JAR. We seriously doubt if Barbara would mention JAR but if you should hear those initials you can nod your head and smile in that knowing way.

Now the tried and trues for fine jewelry such as Harry Winston, Tiffany's, and Shreve, Crump and Low's, Graff, Van Cleef & Arpel (famous in Paris) and Cartier mostly will be in your larger cities and you should know them well. Besides beautiful jewelry, they also carry accessories for your home to help start those antiques and collectibles for the family heirlooms. If you are lucky enough to shop in NYC, do not miss Ivanka Trump's lovely, lovely jewelry. Too breathtaking! You just have to see it to believe it. She understands what well bred women want, period.

As we said earlier, we do not recommend tons of gold bracelets and chains. Use some restraint here but a few do look great for day-time wear. Remember one never wants to look like a Gypsy, a Vegas "tart" or like you just returned from Mardi Gras! Do we need to paint you a picture? Please, ladies, think again, for it is all about image! We would think this would go without saying but the same holds true for our SOF men. Those days are "way over" of looking like a Texas oil trader! We can hear people snickering now and whispering, "Is he a Pimp?" We have warned you! Now don't disappoint us at the School of Flaunt.

Continuing on, lest you forget always have suitable watch wear. As mentioned in our wardrobe lesson, you can never go wrong with a gold Rolex President for day wear and a diamond Cartier for cozy nights on the town. This is good advice for both sexes. Don't want to pay those hefty prices? Well students, we have mentioned before you can always go to an auction. As long as the watch does not have large amounts of jewels on it and no famous provenance, i.e., belonged to a famous person, great buys can be found. Rule of thumb here: stick to watches that do not have multiple functions to perform plus the previous points and the price will be lower in most cases. If in doubt, remember this: "Any fool should know you wear gold with tweeds and platinum with evening wear!" Allegedly the former Duchess of Windsor gave us these helpful words to live by. Heed them well, students, heed them well ... now go get your name on Christie's auction list.

For those of you who don't have a good jeweler, find one! He or she is worth their own weight in gold. Never wear jewelry that is labeled "gold fill" or has inferior quality stones. Others might not discern the difference, but you will know and so will your insurance agent! Word could get around town ... think of this awful scenario ... the front page of the local newspaper reads: "Smith Estate Robbed! $500 worth of Costume Jewelry Taken! This would be your worst nightmare! How could you look your friends, relatives and neighbors in the face? If this regrettable experience should happen it is time to think quickly before you could easily be ostracized from local society for being a fraud! Call your friends immediately and tell them about the unfortunate robbery and how lucky you were that the "good jewelry was in the safe deposit box at the bank." Or try this, "thank God, the home safe is so large and cemented into place they couldn't break into it or move it." Or lastly, "thank God, we have the safe room that we can hide in because we keep our true collectables, the important art work and jewels there." Great saving of face in those trusty statements!

And just so you don't think that we are obsessing about our jewelry, for those of you not familiar with Indian Weddings, please note how the gracious families there bestow upon the Bride "suites" of gold and precious stones. Many dress changes are made for these jewelry displays! Replete with week long parties and celebrations, but we will talk more about this in Lesson Seventeen, concerning Weddings.

Before we dismiss jewelry, as we spoke about earlier, any estate pieces should be coveted and passed on. If you don't have any, start some heirlooms today! Your jeweler will have private showings. So much fun to go into the back private showing rooms and be presented with trays of jewelry to select from! Makes us feel tingly just thinking about it!

You should also make yourself apprised of the finer auction houses. New York, Chicago and Los Angeles have offices for Christie's and Sotheby's. Be on their mailing lists and mark your calendars for the wonderful jewel auctions in the fall in New York. Top Art Auctions are great fun, too and we'll talk about that later in more detail … oh, the people you will meet and the times you will have … and who cares if this $100,000 Cartier bracelet was previously worn by "a Lady?" It might be that great story that they will all love to hear. No one is above a little titillating story! Inquiring minds want to know. Enjoy being the center of attention.

****

Probably some of you at this point are saying, "I can't afford thousands of dollars on jewelry." Here is another **Flaunt Fiscal Tip**: Buy a few wonderful pairs of earrings, a great watch and a spectacular cocktail ring. Then for other occasions you can sneak in some cubic zirconia fake diamond jewelry. Horrors! SOF is recommending fakes here? Yes we are, only if you can't afford to fill your jewelry box with designer jewelry. Listen up students; if you are wearing enough of the real stuff most people will assume that it is all real and who's to tell them? Not you! Be very careful though when choosing costume jewelry, now known as Fashion jewelry. You can pull this off if you choose wisely and mingle it oh so carefully with the real thing and we must admit that some of it is really fun and can set off an outfit nicely.

Lastly, there are many new jewelry designers that are making terrific statements with Fashion jewelry. Whether it be an enamel designed necklace or beaded bracelets from a third world country, they can be a great statement for supporting new talent and the less fortunate! Please remember, NO PLASTIC! Now happy shopping!!!

Here are some of the top jewelers in the country. Stop in their showrooms and get to know them immediately! We bow down to their greatness! Tiffany, Cartier, Graff, Bulgari, Fred Joaillier, Gump's, David Webb, Neil Lane, Harry Winston, Fred Leighton, Ivanka Trump and Van Cleef and Arpel.

Don't forget Neiman Marcus which is in most major cities. They can be a great source for some new talent that can turn into future collectibles. Remember the name Victor Veylan. He can be found at Neiman's. Victor's cuff bracelets are to die for! Think bold! And we have found another interesting talent, Donna Vock. Have you ever thought that exotic woods and Tahitian pearls or ebony wood and diamonds would make great combinations? Well Donna has done it. Make an appointment with her soon! Both Donna and Victor are trés manifique!

**Flaunt Fashion Tip**: Famous designer, Coco Chanel was known for wearing two cuffs at the same time. One on her right wrist and one on her left. One can never have too many cuffs!

**Flaunt Fashion News**: If you don't want to wear your diamonds you can have them on your phone now! Phones encrusted with diamonds will be out hopefully soon. A prototype has been seen and prices start at $50,000. You do get a dock with speakers and a USB port with that. As well you should for $50,000!

**\*\*\*\***

Proceeding along we come to furs. This is a very "sensitive" topic and below is our advice to those of you who still wear fur and those that do not. Please note that we also discuss coats made of wool and cashmere and how to donate your furs to the Humane Society. Wearing or non-wearing of fur is a personal decision and SOF respects all points of view. Therefore, continuing on …

Always spend wisely when it comes to furs. Custom designer please if at all possible! Don't waste time with second-rate furriers. In our humble opinion, American made furs are still the best in comparison to some European made furs. We would like to add here that if you are on a cruise and plan to be stopping in Athens, Greece, it is a furrier's Mecca. The prices are great and the styles are very chic. So do plan to do some shopping while there.

It is important to remember you do get what you pay for when it comes to furs. Have you ever seen those newspaper ads for fur sales at the local convention center or Holiday Inn? Well, we are here to tell you that yes you can get a bargain but guess what? Within a year you will probably be handing your car keys to the valet at your favorite restaurant and while getting out of the car you will hear that wonderful ripping sound, as your sleeve separates from the shoulder of that so-called great bargain mink. Think about this, ladies! You now have to frantically take off your coat, while it is possibly –10 degrees below zero in Chicago, because you don't want someone to see your ripped fur. Then you have to check this coat; my God, if the coat check person sees this and you know they will, your reputation will be tarnished and smeared! Trust us if you don't think that they talk about the customers you are very, very, very naive. Remember students, pay for a knock off or a convention fur and you will get what you paid for. It can turn into a nightmare of tackiness, replete with excess shedding and the sleeves or back splitting! You have been forewarned, students. Total Flaunt Flop!

Here is a little story about furs. One of our famous entertainment Diva's got on the plane. Her fur coat was ankle length but it zipped off at the knees for a daytime look. Alexandra recognized immediately that this was not mink it was "sable" and rushed through the cabin to tell the rest of the crew so that they could all come up to First Class and "subtly" paw the famous Diva's coat in the closet. Now tell us that people don't recognize quality and they do talk among themselves. In retrospect does she feel sorry for doing that? Just a little but who knew and who even remembers! As we said above, remember staff are going to touch your fur and they do talk.

For those of you who are worried about traveling with your fur. Don't be! That is the beauty of fur. It can be rolled up, scrunched and sat on. Just take it, shake it out and you are good to go. Get wet in a little snow who cares? Shake off the water from your coat, hang it up to dry and voilà, it is still ready to wear.

****

Now if unsure about what to wear and when, here are our rules for SOF fur etiquette. Sheared varieties for casual wear, marketing and sporting events. More elaborate showstoppers for evenings. Simple! We would hope that this would be common sense but we have seen otherwise.

Final thoughts on furs: remember also please enter right before the curtain goes up on Act I and you, too will have your moment in the spotlight! For rainy and cold days, a mink lined raincoat is a wonderful idea. Yes, it will have to probably be custom made but you will be ever so chic when running your errands or shopping on Fifth Avenue, Madison Avenue or the Miracle Mile. Please remember that we recommend sable for after six and special daytime occasions. Add a pretty red fox throw for your Rolls Royce and you are set for the coming season but then with heated seats that might be overkill. Save the fur throw for that evening carriage ride around your estate. Lastly, need we say rabbit is only cute on someone under the age of 12.

**** 

SOF does not recommend furs for men! We feel it is, shall we say, only appropriate for Rap stars, if even then. No one else can pull it off! No one! We can not give out the name here but we actually saw a politico type, years ago in the Chicago airport, wearing a mink coat. Talk about a surreal picture. This not to be named person is out in the public championing the poor and is seen in a mink coat. Not bright, not politically correct, and fortunately for all of us now, this not to be identified person seems to have gotten over this really appalling stage of life. There have not been any recent sightings of this poor behavior.

In closing on this topic, we would think that this is a given and we would not have to mention it, but just in case, fur coats made of any endangered species would never appear on our backs or even in our friends closets! Shun those individuals from your life that would go on hunting safaris in Africa and brag about killing any endangered species. They are strictly persona non grata! Enough said!

**** 

Now we know some of you for personal convictions would never wear fur which SOF has absolutely no problems with. A wonderful wool or cashmere coat from a top designer can also take you through life. Picture a gorgeous cashmere shawl thrown over one shoulder or wrapped around both. Of course color coordinate this with your outfit. That look does get a big SOF recommendation! Then there is always a coat or wrap made out of satin or velvet. Gorgeous you will be in that look, too!

Don't forget for the evening, to dress up that wrap or coat, please consider a jeweled brooch for the collar or place it on your shoulder.

If you want to keep them on their toes put that lovely little gold and diamond bee or butterfly pin on the cuff of your coat. Cuff you say? Yes, you too are a Diva of style and remember "quiet" money that starts new trends.

****

We must take the time here to elaborate on the topic of cashmere. Remember these two things must be on the label, either 100% Cashmere or Made in Scotland. What is cashmere? It is the hair on the underbelly of the Mongolian goat. Yes, you did read that right. One Mongolian goat "sheds" enough hair over four years to make only one sweater. It will be warm, light in weight and the softest sweater or scarf you will ever feel. We did say look for made in Scotland but Loro Piana which is an Italian company with a mill outside of Milano has it own herd of goats in Mongolia and has recently introduced a collection of baby cashmere from young "kids" as in baby goats. These sweaters run around $1,000 and coats/wraps for $5,000. Then you can look at the Chicago based company called Queen of Cashmere. Each of their sweaters is specifically designed just for you complete with your own personal monogram and made in Scotland. There are blends making for less costly products but they will also lack the ultimate soft feeling that makes cashmere so wonderful. But buying at the lower ends can still give you a classic look. Another **Flaunt Fiscal Tip**—Remember it is really best to dry clean not hand wash. Dry cleaning will keep your cashmere looking like new! Enjoy those chilly days and nights now in that wonderful cashmere!

****

So you have decided not to wear fur anymore; what to do with those old furs that you might have purchased or inherited? Picture a baby raccoon who has been orphaned. The baby is snuggled into a fur and is quiet and content. Rehabilitating orphaned animals so that they can be released back into the wild is not easy. They have to be kept quiet and handled as infrequently as possible by humans. During the first few days it is critical in relieving stress and that is where a fur coat comes to play. The Humane Society has a program for donated furs called Coats for Cubs (coatsforcubs.org) that distributes coats, stoles and jackets to wildlife rehabilitators. If you are not comfortable wearing furs, please think about donating them for a wonderful cause. SOF "does" give their seal of approval to anything that helps the less fortunate whether it be man or beast. We would like to suggest now that you run to your closets and place your furs in a sturdy box or a small padded envelope for small items. If you would like to receive a letter of thanks please include your mailing address or e-mail requesting an acknowledgement.

Donations can be sent to:
>
> The Humane Society of the United States of America
> 2100 L. St. N.W.
> Washington, D.C. 20037
> Attention: Coats for Cubs

For those of you in New England, the Cape Wildlife Center in Barnstable, Massachusetts, is a recipient of furs from the Humane Society. The Humane Society has also partnered with the Buffalo Exchange. No they do not raise Buffalo. This is a resale clothing chain where you may drop off your fur items. Small aside here, there is also a tax deduction up to $5,000. Then you start treading on thin ice with the IRS, students. None of you will look good in an orange jumpsuit! (Please refer back to Lesson One for SOF thoughts on resale shopping.)

# Lesson Three Quiz

1. What is an unacceptable stone to wear?
   a. Under one carat
   b. Something you have a hard time lifting your hand when wearing
   c. A stone that could possibly blind someone for life
   d. Emerald, Ruby, Diamond

ANSWER: A


2. Is bigger usually better when buying jewels?
   a. ALWAYS! ALWAYS! ALWAYS!
   b. Never
   c. None of the above

ANSWER: A – Shame on you if you didn't answer A.


3. What should you do if you inherit a stone smaller than a carat?
   a. Immediately trade up
   b. Purchase a second and turn them into studs for casual wear
   c. Give to a small child
   d. Sell and donate the money to your favorite charity
   e. Any of the above
   f. None of the above

ANSWER: E


4. What is certified Blackglama?
   a. A world-renowned boxer who shall remain nameless

    b. An International Secret Organization
    c. Certification that your mink garment is made of original Blackglama mink pelts.
    d. Janet Jackson

ANSWER: C – But Janet is totally glam, too!

5. When a jeweler has a "Bespoke" offering, what does this mean?
    a. Someone has "dibs" or hold on a piece of jewelry
    b. They will remake or design a special piece just for you.
    c. A piece of jewelry resembling a bicycle wheel
    d. Never heard of it!

ANSWER: B – Have we taught you nothing? If you missed this you must go back to Lesson One and start all over again!

6. What is the Tudor Rose?
    a. A Rock Group
    b. A Perfume
    c. English Royalty
    d. A life-size diamond rose brooch

ANSWER: D – This was a slight trick question, students, for we did not mention it in this lesson but it makes you think!

7. Who, what, or where is JAR?
    a. A kind of jar used to "can fruits or vegetables"
    b. Newest make of a private jet
    c. Slang for Jakarta, Indonesia
    d. Joel Arthur Rosenthal

ANSWER: D – If you missed this reread this lesson immediately!

8. Who are Fred and Harry?
    a.  Old Vaudeville Comedy Act
    b.  Uncles that you don't want anyone to meet
    c.  Your new best friends
    d.  Fred Leighton and Harry Winston
    e.  C & D

ANSWER: E – Again if you didn't know these names immediately, shame on you students, reread this lesson because you have flunked!

9. Want to earn some extra credits here for graduation? Memorize the following:

    a.  Rojtman Diamond, weight 107.46 carats. Fancy yellow, cushion cut. Origins shrouded in mystery.
    b.  Golden Maharaja, 65.57 carats. Pear-shaped diamond of fancy dark orange-brown color. Allegedly, previously owned by one of the wealthiest Maharajas in the 1930s.

Above great information for "cocktail chatter." You are encouraged to do more research on these and other jewels with interesting histories.

## LESSON FOUR:
### Votre Maison

"All Gated Communities are not Created Equal!"

DOES MARGARET RUSSELL know where you live? She certainly should! Why? Because she is the new editor-in-chief of Architectural Digest, the most prestigious interiors magazine in the United States. Keep up students! Margaret will now put her indomitable "flaunt flair" on AD which we are all looking forward to. But we must take a moment to recognize Paige Rense, the former editor of Architectural Digest, who brought us so many hours of pleasure. Thank you Paige and enjoy your retirement but we know you will not be relegated to the back pages!

Now what caught Paige's eye in the past and most likely will still be something that Margaret looks for is not a "Crib" with fake fur throws! A true SOF home is full of flaunt and has some of the following:

1.  A top drawer Address or Zip Code. If your town does not have a Society Hill start one!

2.  Your property must have an outstanding view. Whether that be a picturesque garden, 1,000 acres of Kentucky bluegrass, the Atlantic, the Pacific, Great Lakes or skyline of a magnificent city. Always have a view! Remember here we did say you may have a

wonderful garden and that could be the easiest way of getting that view. Ever hear of landscapers?

**Note**: All plastic decorative items are FORBIDDEN to be used in your gardens; e.g., pink flamingos, bird houses, Bambi and Thumper, and the dreaded gnome.

3. This leads us to choosing an Interior Designer. Needless to say their job is usually easier when you have a view but basically their most important work is to introduce you to the elegance and taste of a truly unique home. Don't decorate piecemeal or skimp. Nothing is worse than a twenty room estate with no living room furniture. Pity the poor home that is decorated by objects from The Dollar Store or your local Assistance League. Perish the thought about using those sources for decorating ideas! Try never to think in terms of small. Not that small can't be elegant too! We will make an exception for major city condos and apartments: e.g., New York City, Chicago or San Francisco with the right address.

Very important students: look to frequenting estate sales where you can attain more heirlooms. We do not mean "yard sales" and absolutely no "dumpster diving" either! Chances of you finding anything of real value are a million in one shot. The thrill of the chase, wearing a hat, sunglasses and disguise to rifle through someone's trash with the hopes of finding an antique are just not worth it. Heaven forbid you are seen by someone's staff who might be at this yard sale and they recognize you. We feel like a "case of the bends" is starting at just thinking about this entire scenario.

If you bring this up to a prospective designer for them to do, well some might, but we seriously doubt that most would like to spend their weekends going to garage sales.
Don't be surprised if this is their reaction: first we can see their eyes rolling up into the back of their head as you ask them to go to yard sales. Then they are frantically closing their portfolio of

previous jobs, tripping over your ugly little coffee table that has your Grandmother's doilies on it and have started running for the nearest exit screaming for someone to help them find the front door! After they get back to their office they are trying to make up their minds if they had just awoken from a nightmare or did it really happen? When they decide it was for real they will be on the phone ASAP. Wait until this gets around the decorating community. No one will return your calls!

Now if that isn't enough to make you stop and think, picture this awful scene: the local police stopping you while you are rifling through someone's trash cans at night for a non-existent treasure. Remember they have to write up reports that usually end up in your local paper to fill space but in this case it will probably make some headlines because of your status in the community: "Socialite Caught Rifling Through Upscale Neighborhood's Trash Cans!" When asked what she was doing she replied, "Oh dumpster diving for goodies. It is so much fun." Please will someone get us a glass of champagne and a pillow to relax on while we try to recoup from that ugly little picture! Your reputation is simply ruined, you might as well move out of town!

But we have digressed: back to choosing a designer, you may try a budding new one but be very careful here and if unsure stick with the tried and true designers with pedigrees that resemble: Albert Hadley & Sister Parish, Billy Baldwin, Barbara Barry, Mark Hampton, Barry Dixon, Joel Woodard, Mary Douglas Drysdale or Mario Buatta. They are worth the investment and we are sure their designs will speak School of Flaunt.

**Note**: Do not limit yourself to a designer from your city. Talented designers travel the world working and beautifying with the best! They should be willing to go to Timbuktu to research and purchase for you. Don't settle for a designer who doesn't have credentials such as: graduating from Parsons School of Design, notable names of homes they have rescued from the poor taste of previous designers and homes that you have actually seen "inside." The proof is in the pudding students! And never be fooled with a portfolio of pictures that they used from previous issues of AD that are actually someone else's work. Trust us it does happen!

**Flaunt Fiscal Tip**: For those of you who still seem to think that you can decorate on your own and piece meal, we would like to suggest one of our favorite books. <u>101 Things I Hate About Your House</u> by noted Interior Designer, James Swan. It is a true eye opener and hopefully the pictures alone will save you thousands of dollars from poor decorating! Take a peak and see how you fare in the design world.

4.  Investing in your designer leads us to furnishings. If in doubt, stick to period pieces such as 18th century Chinese Chippendale or Country French. Throw in a touch of antiques to show your taste and refinement. A crystal chandelier will always impress and they do look so lovely in the evening on dim. Romantic dinner for two or dinner party for the Society pages? Either way Flaunt Fabulous. Now picture your dining table with a fabulous chandelier over it. It will be great for that AD picture! Speaking of lighting, don't forget you will need some great lamps for your other rooms. We suggest a few vintage Marbro lamps or find that perfect base and turn it into a gorgeous new lamp. Oh, you are so discriminating now.

Least we say, never, never, be cutesy! Cutesy might possibly work for your beach house or a cabin but we have found that this technique of decorating usually leads to clutter and clutter is TACKY students! Example: Think kitchen counter tops with lots of ceramic chickens placed throughout, mixed in between too many small appliances. We need Valium and lots of bed rest just picturing that! This is the perfect description of clutter and totally tacky or as we prefer to call it, FLAUNT FLOP!

Now don't hurt yourself rushing to the kitchen to remove those chickens! Please put the small appliances out of sight and we might humor you with keeping one large Rooster. Thank you! If you are still in doubt visit the Winterthur Museum in Delaware. The DuPont family had impeccable taste and there is no clutter anywhere! Please note that even George Washington's china is neatly stacked and displayed.

Remember these names! Baker, Henredon, Kindle and Karges. No, this is not a circus act! Memorize those names for they are top drawer makers of furniture that have been producing "new" furniture that will someday be someone's antique. And speaking of new, Judson Rothschild is a newer name on the scene for furniture design. Judson's furniture has a rich patina that gives it old-world charm. Remember the warm patina of age can still be achieved without buying antiques. Please for clarification, students, when we say "new furniture," we are not suggesting unfinished pine. Heaven forbid that won't even do for a log cabin. Plus staining will ruin your manicure. Imagine, you are in your basement or garage staining and the door bell rings, where do you go with the brush and old clothes before receiving guests?

**Flaunt Fiscal Tip:** The founder of a dot-com business was having his home decorated. The designer was showing him pictures of vases and he asked, "how much is each one?" "Well," the decorator said, "this one is $500 and that one is $1000." The man being obviously one of the sharper knives in the rack thought to himself, "I bet I can get the same thing on eBay for a lot less." Yes, students, need we remind you the rich do not throw their money away. So he went on eBay and guess what? There were the vases for $50 and $100. So use your ingenuity when decorating. Bet you were all thinking that he probably went belly up with the dot-com bust. No, he was smart as we said and sold out his shares for millions earlier! Retired at 45 in the comfort of a 9,600 sq. ft. home on 19 acres with a pool, tennis court and fruit orchard. Lesson to be learned students, never be greedy and you will sell at the right time.

**Flaunt Fiscal Tip**: Earlier we mentioned estate sales. Very, very important here students. You can purchase a beautiful circa 1920 oil on canvas, depending on the artist and size for approximately $5000, whereas, if you went to a high end gallery, you would pay two or three times that amount! So get on those web sites for auctions and start checking out the furniture, art work, silver and china. These are great sites for rugs, books and crystal, in short, all the makings of a "very fine and important home." A quote from auctioneer and appraiser Stuart Holman from Cincinnati.

**Last Flaunt Fiscal Tip on furnishings**: Do not go to antique stores other than to check out the merchandise, unless you have very deep pockets and then who cares, enjoy! For our antique novices, these wonderful establishments are a great way to learn. Check out books from your local library and visit your local Barnes and Noble or Borders to start educating yourself. Remember it would be nice to be able to talk about something other an old episode of Ugly Betty or whatever! Nothing against Betty, mind you and we do miss that show. Small aside here, remember an ugly duckling can turn into a swan. Never give up hope!

5. Now if you are building obviously you must have a fine architect. Interview many and see their plans of previous homes they have designed. You will also have to decide on a theme. Stony Brook architect Gary Lawrance, an architectural model builder, is an expert on the Gilded Age mansions. Lawrance says, "that while estates were actually built in many styles, from Georgian to French, Italianate and Spanish models, tall columns became iconic emblems of wealth and power." He continues with, "if you want to say important country estate, then you have Greek columns. It's pretty much what people like to think of as the classical mansion."

We at SOF say, "even if Greek columns are too much for you, remember every home has a theme whether it be a French Chateaux, an English Tudor, a Mediterranean Villa or New England Cape Cod." Your home should reflect your taste while also being a place that your friends and family can gather and enjoy too. Be careful students, do not turn your home into a theme park though. Those are so tiring! Example: think Neverland as in Michael Jackson. We do not want to speak ill of the deceased but trains and Wild Animal parks on estates are not our thing. Sounds something like a Saudi Prince might do though.

Continuing on: please don't forget that every well-planned estate would have any or all of the following: 10-12 foot ceilings "minimum," French doors leading to a spacious terrace, traditional mahogany or walnut paneling, European tile, travertine or wide plank wood floors, a bath for every bedroom and of course a library for your selection of leather-bound books! If at all possible consider your own pub room and wine cellar, game room with private theater and popcorn machine, bowling alley plus a private gym where you can meet your trainer. Ladies don't forget to add in the plans your own personal beauty salon for those private shall we say, "upkeep appointments." Think they don't incorporate that in fine estates, we've seen them! NOTE: The library can make an interesting room for intimate catered dinners.

Don't forget when planning your baths that the master suite should include its own environment spa, replete with sauna, dressing and sitting rooms. Be prepared to drop anywhere from $100,000 to $200,000 or even more on your master bath alone. You are worth this, students!

**Flaunt Flash News**: Famed Harrods in London is selling a bathtub for $790,000 that is carved from a single block of crystal which was found in the Amazon! This "flaunt fabulous" tub is designed by an Italian firm called Baldi. It took six months to chip this crystal into a beyond-gorgeous soaking tub. Yes six months, students! Ah, relaxing in your $1,000,000 tub, remember duty, shipping and installation but oh my how it is going to feel! Worth every little cent, don't you think? Unfortunately they only had two of them and these do sell fast. Probably you are not in luck but Harrods is resourceful and might be able to get another one made for you.

Most importantly other rooms in your home should be left to your imagination, hobbies and needs. We do highly recommend if possible to have a guest wing or "preferably" a separate and charming guest house. Trust us you will appreciate your house guests much more that way! Remember the old adage, house guests and fish after three days go bad. (Please refer to Lesson Five about entertaining and house guests.)

For a truly finishing touch please include an elevator in the plans since your home will probably have three floors. Neighbors of ours had 4 floors, they definitely needed their elevator. Plus, we hate doing steps unless we are exercising. Puh-leese, no escalator that is ridiculous! And lastly, if you are so inclined or not, SOF recommends for your grounds: tennis court, putting green, skeet or trap range, croquet courts, stables, gardens to stroll in and of course, a pool with "pool house" and whirlpool go without saying. Remember for children's parties a bowling alley in the lower level of your home can be fun, too! Ah the good life, pamper yourself and entertain in style!

Now if any of you ever have the opportunity to see a home in Beverly Park, Los Angeles or are just being invited to one now, RSVP yes immediately! It is totally amazing, with one palace-like home next to another, it easily could be described as Billionaires' Row. Anything under 15,000 sq. ft. is actually cozy. Cozy we say because other houses in this extremely private community for Hollywood potentates, business tycoons and sports stars are much larger. How large you ask? Most are 20,000 sq. ft. to 30,000 sq.

ft. or even in a few cases more than 40,000. Better put a beeper on the children to find them or under constant supervision by their Nanny.

We heard that when the wife of a well-known political type and society grand dame was visiting in a certain 11,000 sq ft. home she said, "I didn't know they built houses like this anymore." Now calm yourself students for that rude comment. It was an unfortunate slip of the tongue which we are not condoning. In her defense because we know she was always the lady, you must remember she was from generations of money and socialized with the movers and shakers of the world. Mansions and castles were not strangers to her and probably 11,000 sq. ft. did seem a tad small. Hopefully she wrote a lovely thank you note to the hostess and sent her a large bouquet of flowers! Remember, students, if you should ever be in this situation and embarrass yourself send flowers and a note full of flattery about the evening at the very least!

The point we are trying to make students is that you don't have to have the largest home in the neighborhood. Your address, Zip Code or area is what is important. Remember, if you haven't really made it big, our goal here is to help you move up the social ladder anyway.

We would like to recommend to all of our younger readers that in our humble opinion "think real estate." Yes, through buying and selling you will be able to eventually live in that SOF neighborhood. Think big and you will most likely make it big. Think small, students, and you will most likely remain in that non-SOF neighborhood.

Now we can hear you saying right now to yourself, "real estate, you want me to invest in real estate." Yes, we want you to at the very least think about purchasing real estate. Why? This is very important, because a great piece of land or a prestigious neighborhood with the right Zip code will always make you money in the long run! Buy in a so-so neighborhood because you are really getting a deal, which is not a bad idea for a starter home or rental and you will never have the assurance that your investment is safe. If you can afford a little more and you buy that really small home in a great neighborhood, trust us you'll make more money in the short term as well as into the future. The old adage in real estate always holds true, LOCATION, LOCATION, LOCATION. Remember sometimes the land becomes more valuable than the home. Think tear downs! Always be planning for the future.

6.  Do hire a landscape architect, as little problems and alas large ones can be either taken care of right from the beginning or redone, as in the case of an older estate home. Add a dash of original art work and sculptures on the lawn and presto you look almost a good as Longwood Gardens. Never heard of Longwood? Well, get thyself on a plane now and go to Kennett Square, Pennsylvania, outside of Philadelpia. Approximately 1,050 acres awaits you and we see a magnificent greenhouse in your future after you see their's. This should go without saying but always have your cabana curtains and towels coordinated with the veranda furnishings. Students, your pool house and guest house should never be second thoughts. Remember AD photos! Lastly, add flowers everywhere and you are ready for guests.

Lest we forget your landscape architect should always plan a cutting garden. Why? Because flowers are simply a must in every room and they are expensive.

**Flaunt Fiscal Tip**: To cut down on expenses and also have fresh flowers at the ready a cutting garden is a must. Think Lalique or Waterford bud vases or larger bowls filled with fresh flowers. Gorgeous!

You say you don't know how to arrange flowers? Not to worry, you just need to take some courses. However if a cutting garden is impossible to have, especially if you reside in a luxury condo, then we would like to suggest high end silk arrangements. This can cost you anywhere from $500 and up depending on size and containers, but the wonderful thing about these arrangements is that they keep for years and years and never go out of style. The truly high end silks are so realistic that you will have to touch them to see the difference. Decades ago, high end silks were hand made in Italy. Today they are imported mostly from the Far East but with good research you can find a store who carries them and will design your arrangement for you. Don't quibble over the price because this will end up being a work of art and quibbling can be so tedious. You aren't buying a car. Quit saying "is this your best price."

**Flaunt Fiscal Tip**: Remind yourself that these arrangements will end up being a veritable bargain vs. fresh from the florist. Do the math! Sorry we are not recommending lower end stores for floral arrangements. The difference in quality and look is staggering.

Just a little true story, students. We spoke about your cutting garden and recently a friend told us a story about how a hostess was able to use hers so successfully. She was having a "High Tea" for about 40 of her women friends. Tea replete with linens, china and silver. Lots of finger sandwiches, scones and clotted cream filled the dining room table. Even Martha Stewart would have been impressed. And that is not easy!

Champagne and Mimosas were also flowing as well as the tea. Slightly non-traditional but ever so much fun! The individual tables for the guests all had a different theme, each with their own colored linens, teapots with matching sugar and creamers and every table had a clever name. Think Princess Diana, Madonna to HRH Queen Elizabeth. Very beautiful and festive to say the least but here is where we get to the flowers. The hostess who was having the tea had wonderful floral arrangements on every table. She had actually gone out in the morning, cut lavender, roses, daisies and much more from her own garden. All of her vases on the tables just popped with color. The guests were overheard to say, "her flowers are lovely and I think they came from her beautiful garden." Just a small FLAUNT FLORAL tidbit here, but worth all of that gardening. She added a Hat Contest to the gathering and believe me there was a lot of FLAUNT FASHION in that room. Now we must add, as usual have a great caterer and plenty of help so that you can enjoy the tea too. You do want to sparkle and we don't want it to be from perspiration from you serving your guests. You are the hostess not the help!

7. Every grand home has a "Moniker" … take heed and carefully think about the naming of your residence! Wouldn't you prefer to have your friends and guests arrive at the front gate and see a lovely plaque with the name of your home on it versus just some numbers and an address. Really how boring! Think history here, students. All of the fine estates, southern plantations and horse farms are named.

You will find if your home is named that people will start referring to it as such. Example: the local florist when he is telling his delivery person where to go, "Take these to Hummingbird Nest." Or when someone is giving directions, i.e., "Go two miles and when you get to Hummingbird Nest make a left-hand turn." And just think, students, from here to eternity it will always be referred to by that name. No we do not jest. We have found that even when one moves, the community will always refer to the original name even if the new owners rename it. You will have left your permanent mark!

No matter how humble, nothing says School of Flaunt as a "monogrammed home." From cottage to castle, named homes are just in a higher realm of real estate. Think: Rose Cottage, Hummingbird Nest, The Elms, Calumet Farms, etc.

How do you decide on a name? Select some obvious characteristics of the landscape or architecture and expand. Don't use your name! Smith Ranch, really, students, so terribly de classé. If you must use your name try something like, Taylor Hill. Obviously you own the entire hill. Hopefully more than a mere acre! Now remember, once a name has been selected, think of the monogramming possibilities: e.g., towels, linens, robes, slippers, stationary, calling cards, silver, china, the cheque book.

Oh, the list is endless here. Picture that lovely party with desserts served with your home's monogram on them. Or even better yet, have your guests leave with chocolates with the appropriate monogram. Watch the reaction! Just a little something for them to remember that fabulous evening. We can almost guarantee that they will all be dreaming that night of traveling the road to riches and revelry which all started with your lovely plaque or signage. Small point here: don't offer your guests left-overs from the dinner to take home. They aren't family! We are cringing at that picture of little baggies. Puh-leese! You are not a restaurant. The next thing we know you will be taking lessons as to how to wrap up left-overs in foil that look like a Swan. STOP!

But let us return to your home's "moniker." Just think if you sent out invitations like this: "A Weekend at The Elms." Flaunt Fabulous to say the least. We are sure you will receive rave reviews by all who are lucky enough to be sent that invitation. Now get thyself to your local post office and set up your Post Office Box number with your named estate. And please do not forget that you also need a new checking account. Why you ask? Because everyone who is anyone has a checking account with the name of their estate on it and underneath that name it simply says, Household Account. Think we are jesting here with you? Oh no, our School of Flaunt devotees, it is done all of the time. The local shops will recognize that estate name and one knows they never will ask for identification because they also recognize you and your staff. They realize you might be sending your driver later to pick up your latest purchases and are ready to store said items until then. Remember you never "schlep" around with bags! These are just all suggestions for your School of Flaunt ammunition. Just lock and reload!

**Note**: If you have been invited to said home with a "moniker," please refer to Lesson Six on Manners and Etiquette for Guest Rules of the Road. It goes without saying that only the best will be asked to a Country Weekend. If you fail this, kiss your social calendar goodbye. Remember: Fish and House Guests SMELL after Three Days! Heed this well and our other pointers, students. You will thank us.

8. Let's say you have finally arrived, done your homework and pleased the most discerning host/hostess. You want to reciprocate. Be it ever so NOT modest, a vacation home is a must! Vacation homes can be purchased in any of these areas for SOF devotees: Newport, Rhode Island; Nantucket, Massachusetts; Palm Beach, Del Ray Beach, Naples or Long Boat Key, Florida; Lake Tahoe or Palm Desert, California; Hawaii, any of the islands are acceptable; Hilton Head, South Carolina; Pinehurst, North Carolina; Taos, New Mexico and always, Aspen and Vail, Colorado! Enjoy your vacation, you earned it!! The house guest shoe is on the other foot, so to speak and now you will be the entertaining "wonder" of the resort world.

Remember here is where you can enjoy a smaller home or condo. This is "your" get away place. We are not recommending that you decorate in poor taste because you might have visitors and friends over, but antiques are not a must. You can do a theme vacation home. Beach, ranch, ski lodge or whatever strikes your fancy. A very important point to remember students is a second home in a vacation area will usually see a healthy increase in price during a boom time but will be the most adversely affected (price wise) if there is a recession. So bearing this thought in mind try to buy during a down time in the economy and pick up that bargain. You can enjoy it for a few years and then eventually sell it for the big bucks and move on. SOF'ers are always planning for the future. We do so love being Fiscally Flaunt.

Every city has its own Upper East Side. Are you living there? ONE LAST TIME, REMEMBER: LOCATION, LOCATION, LOCATION!

**Flaunt Fiscal Tip**: Now that HGTV has hit the airwaves, there is really no excuse not garnering some great design knowledge from certain notable TV Designers. One can envision their own space and gardens brimming with HGTV Design Ideas! We can thank Joe Ruggiero, noted designer, for bringing great design to the masses! We love Joe's Sunbrella Fabrics! So practical for the Pool House.

## Lesson Four Quiz

1. Who are Baker, Knapp & Tubb?
    a. A famous vaudeville team
    b. A brokerage house
    c. An after-dinner liqueur
    d. A world-renowned furniture company
    e. Another slice of heaven

ANSWER: Definitely D & E


2. How should you pick a designer?
    a. The yellow pages
    b. Aunt Tulla's BFF
    c. Town & Country Magazine Endorsement
    d. Architectural Digest Spread
    e. C & D

ANSWER: E – Hopefully we have taught you well!


3. What should every well-planned estate have?
    a. Linoleum flooring
    b. Flocked wallpaper
    c. Smoked mirrors on the walls and ceiling
    d. Mahogany paneling, 12' ceilings, a bath ensuite for every bedroom

ANSWER: D – If you couldn't answer this correctly we give up! Put the book down and go get on your dirt bike for a spin around the corn field.

4. Which of the following are not suitable areas for vacation homes?
    a. Newark, NJ
    b. Peoria, IL
    c. Toledo, OH
    d. Fargo, ND
    e. Needles, CA
    f. All of the above

ANSWER: F

5. Which of the following are not High End Appliance Manufacturers?
    a. Miele
    b. Wolf
    c. Fox
    d. Viking
    e. Sub Zero

ANSWER: C – This was not covered, but shows that there is so much to learn, dear students, when it comes to good kitchen design.

6. What should a Gated Community have?
    a. A Guard House that is manned 24/7!
    b. A private golf course
    c. If on the water, each home should have its own private dock
    d. Air strip for airplanes
    e. $450 space rent for your double wide including trash pick up
    f. A, B & C

ANSWER: F – Air strips can be way too noisy for the neighbors. Think John Travolta with his commercial plane—YIKES! If the area should have landing rights for Helicopters make sure they have restricted hours. If you answered E you have just been thrown out of the School of Flaunt!

7. What should you look for when purchasing a home?
   a. Location
   b. Zip Code
   c. Address
   d. All of the above

ANSWER: D – If we haven't taught you anything from this Lesson it should be this. Please memorize LOCATION, LOCATION, LOCATION

8. What should every good garden include?
   a. Fountains
   b. Yard art
   c. Gorgeous bird feeders
   d. Plastic Pink Flamingos
   e. Plastic grazing deer
   f. A, B & C

ANSWER: F – Have you learned nothing students. Plastic items should only be seen around your pool in the form of toys for the pool, drinking glasses and plates! We hate PLASTIC, except for flip flops by the pool!

9. Which of the following is a name befitting your Votre' Maison monogram?
   a. High Horse Highway
   b. Big Bucks Ranch
   c. The Elms
   d. Viagra Valley

ANSWER: C – If you missed this one … please re-read Point # 7 and now you must memorize it! No we are not kidding!

10. If some nouveau riche person asks you if they may see all of your
   home, what should you reply?
   a. Yes
   b. I'll get the maid to take you on a tour.
   c. Would you mind taking one of the dogs on a walk while you
      are snooping?
   d. NO daarrrling

ANSWER: D – Now please consult Lesson Six: SOF Attitude,
Manners and Etiquette. Learning the art of saying NO is essential.
This is where you will use your cool stare and cool voice that you have
practiced in the mirror. Remember students we do not want to ever
hear anyone tell us that you were the offending party and asked to see
all of their home. If that should come to our attention your graduation
diploma will be recalled immediately and your name struck from our
list of graduates. We will add here that if it is a house warming party
the Host and Hostess will assume that you would like to see the entire
home. Here is the appropriate occasion where "they" will offer to take
you on a tour.

# LESSON FIVE:
## Entertaining & Staffing
### "The Fine Art of a Soireé"

ENTERTAINING SHOULD BE an enjoyable experience for the best host and hostess as well as the guests! That means you must take several things into account when planning a party. Please note: No one in their cups!! Bad form that one.

First, have plenty of HELP, HELP, HELP! Then decide who you are trying to impress, your family, friends, new neighbors or business associates? You can wow all of them, but we do not recommend combining said groups. Aunt Millie's favorite potato salad can get an "A" with the family but it could literally flunk out with the business "caviar" set. But on second thought, little boiled new organic red skin potatoes filled with caviar and a small dollop of sour cream placed on either side or carefully on the top does make for a delicious new form of potato salad. Yummy! Now aren't you the Flaunt Foodie?

Second, is the party to have a theme: Holiday, Pool, Sporting Event, Sunday Brunch or, just simply the Black Tie Sit Down?

**A little School of Flaunt hint:** If you are having cocktails and an orchestra on the lawn, please do not water your turf for two full days prior. This omits the possibility of your Jimmy Choos sinking into the wet grass. Water your flower beds where needed.

Third, as said earlier have plenty of staff. Any event at your home where you will be entertaining a minimum of 20 people requires a bartender, someone to serve and keep the home tidy and a valet to park cars, even if you do "not" have a long drive. Do you want your guests to have to park their cars on a public street and walk up to your home? We hope not! Remember it could be cold or hot outside, rainy or windy. Puh-leese would you like to fight the elements to come to your affair? Certainly not! That is why you need the valet. Frankly, Alexandra and Cate each find it very aggravating when they have spent hours getting ready and it is all undone in 2 minutes by the elements! Now if they are unhappy, what are those Grande Dames of society thinking!

Fourth, this takes us to the best caterer in town or referred to as "Your Godsend." At the end of the evening you will be thanking the Almighty for him or her. Catering does obviously get the SOF seal of approval, if for no other reason than you can be fully relaxed and spend time with your friends.

Lastly, it does protect your manicure in every case and manicures are not cheap. Subtract the cost of having to redo your manicure and that lowers the catering costs. Then think of the new Chanel outfit being ruined because you were refilling the canape tray. Splash—big oil stain—now doesn't that look attractive on the dress you are wearing while you are chatting up the guests. Not! And we can hear you yelling at your husband, "Tom I need your help in the kitchen, NOW." That screams sophisticated. Not! Just saying students.

**A little School of Flaunt hint:** If you have been having staff problems, it is very chic now to attend cooking schools all over the world. This will prove invaluable when critiquing the caterer or your cook, as well as give you innovative ideas. Now start packing, have a wonderful time at a Flaunt Fancy cooking school and invite your good friends to come along!

Speaking of inviting and a party, it is so entertaining to have the chef come to your home and give private cooking lessons, as everyone sips on some wonderful wine and watches. You pass out the recipes as party favors, sit down and let his people serve all and they do the clean up. How much fun was that and absolutely no work! Please remember to make sure you have checked with the chef for the proper wine pairings. Bon Appetit students!

**Flaunt Flash News:** This just in: A new TV Show called *The Chew* has culinary advice that will not only help you prepare Flaunt Fiscal meals, make healthy dining choices and learn the latest in kitchen trends. Check it out, students!

**\*\*\*\***

Remember this, if your caterer or chef suggests wine pairings that create an unruly havoc on the tongue, fire them immediately and do not recommend them to friends. Wines are to complement the food not ruin it.

Even though we know wines can be subjective to everyone's taste you can still follow certain rules when pairing wine with food. Obviously your heavier red meat dishes should be served with a fuller-bodied red wine such as a Cabernet Savignon, Zinfandel or Merlot. Lighter fare usually goes well with white wine. If the food is acidic with a lemon-based sauce a Pinot Grigio will do nicely. For summer dining with a chicken salad try a dry Riesling. Don't forget that a Chenic Blanc and Sauvignon Blanc usually go well with white fish and that salmon can be paired with a Pinot Noir, Gamay or Sangiovese. FLAUNTILIOUS, for our Flaunt Foodies.

Don't forget this: absolutely no combining of Reds with spicy sea-food for you will probably get a nasty metallic taste on your tongue. This will surely ruin your meal, your dinner party and the entire evening. A terrible way to end a SOF day! And lastly, when pairing wine and cheese or recipes from certain countries to wines, your best bet is to stick with the region that the food and wine both come from. Why do the locals drink their wine with their food? Duh, because obviously over the years they have figured out what tastes the best together. Don't try to reinvent the "wine wheel" here. Wine Wheel … that was a Flaunt Flash!

When in doubt go to the finest wine shop in town and speak with the owner; or at the very least go to the internet for advice.

**Note**: When we are speaking of a wine shop we are not referring to a large "box store" where a 21 year old is handing out advice as to what is a good wine. Please if in doubt consult with either Alexandra or Cate at their blog site, www.schoolofflaunt.com. We will be happy to advise you. Cheers!

Also remember, the staff at the supermarket does not necessarily know the produce. We recently inquired about where they had stocked the shallots. The teenager returns with scallions in her hand. When I told her those were not shallots she said, "Well they told me they were onions." I said, "Yes, a shallot is an onion but all onions are not shallots." At this point I told her to follow me and we found the shallots. A picture is worth a thousand words.

****

Do you want your friends to consider you an Oenophile? Should you be able to hold a conversation with your Sommelier? If you didn't answer yes to both of those questions we have failed at the School of Flaunt. Please pop a Brewski, get out the dirt bike and ride off into the sunset never to return! If your answer was yes to both of them it is time to start your research and stock your wine cellar. Even you teetotalers, this is a must: if you do purchase a home with a wine cellar it is so totally non-SOF to leave it empty. Plus they do look ever so romantic when they are filled. Something titillating about seeing 1,000s of bottles, all beautifully displayed, in a properly chilled room. Love is in the air! Oh, do excuse us we have digressed. (Please consult Lesson Seven for some great vacation spots to learn more about wines around the world.)

Now we will settle the all important question of what is the true drink of School of Flaunt devotees? It is champagne and we are not talking about non-vintage Barefoot Bubbly here. We are proud to announce that we are drinking Armand De Brignac, Ace of Spades Champagne, which is produced in Reims, France. This would also make a beautiful present since it is in a stunning gold bottle, with a real pewter label, packaged in a black wooden gift box and presented in an embroidered velvet bag. Excuse us we are having a School of

Flaunt moment just at the thought of this. Let's take a few seconds here to give thanks, students. Heads bowed.

Could you ask for anything more? We think not since this nectar of the Gods has been served by the Queen of England at her Golden Jubilee Celebration and Jay Z in his Show Me What You Got video. Put those names together and all of a sudden you have a cult following and a hot new champagne that is hard to come by. So when someone says, "Shall we have champagne with our dinner?" You should show off a little flaunt flash and respond, "Yes, let's do have some Ace of Spades." A 750 ML bottle will cost approximately $300 retail at a first class liquor shop. If you can find it at a restaurant get ready to pay the big School of Flaunt bucks but tell your dining partners it is well worth it!

**Flaunt Flash News**: Dallas Mavericks owner Mark Cuban spent $90,000 on a bottle of Armand de Brignac, a.k.a. Ace of Spades celebrating his Mavs win over the Heat to take the NBA Championship in 2011! How big was that bottle?

For further ammo in your School of Flaunt vocabulary tell them that Ace of Spades has previously received a 98 point score from wine critic Jose Penin, 4.9 out of 5 from champagne writer Kare Hallden and 9 out of 10 points from critic Davor Putkovic. Ah yes, we can taste those delicate little bubbles bouncing off of our tongue now. Think, foie gras or salmon on toast points. Possibly soft-shelled crabs on a bed of asparagus and artichokes. We understand Martha has served these with pink champagne! Time for Martha to discover Ace of Spades. So hurry up students, no dawdling, get thyself to the wine shop and order some now! There has to be some grand occasion or dinner for two that you would like to celebrate soon!

****

Now if you would like to throw around some more flaunt chatter for dinner conversation try this. A six liter, gold labeled bottle of Cristal

Brut 1990 named the Methuselah was sold in 2005 at a Sotheby's auction in NY to an undisclosed buyer for $17,625. Rumor has it that it was probably someone in the hip-hop crowd that purchased it? We do not know.

In 2005 a Dom Perignon White Gold Jeroboam in a white, gold, 3 liter bottle sold for $40,000. Happy New Year! But in 1997 a bottle of 1945 Chateau Mouton-Rothschild Jeroboam sold at auction for $114,614. Where will it stop?

And lastly, a bottle of 1787 Chateau Lafitte sold in 1985, in London, for a reported $160,000. Why? Because allegedly it came from Thomas Jefferson's wine cellar (as in President Jefferson) and had Th.J initials etched into the glass bottle. Insanity!

**** 

But we need to be continuing on with entertaining …

Fifth, flowers everywhere! Consider that to be a FLAUNT FLORAL must! Even your 4th of July events should have the proverbial red, white and blue posies. Before you know it each party will be considered a gala by all.

**Another Little Flaunt Fabulous Tip:** small gifts, or favors for each guest to remember the occasion is a nice touch! We know of someone who entertained 200 at a Western-themed party, complete with western band, chuck wagons and horses. All of the guests went home with their own cowboy hat. Cute! Note: this affair was outside of Chicago, not out west where everyone would come wearing their own $500 hat.

Even bigger and better is the debutante who receives a new car at her coming out and also presents new cars to all her sister debs that season! Now that is a gift everyone will remember and one-upmanship is always the way to go if possible. Keep them guessing as to what you'll do to top yourself! We wonder if Oprah got her idea here?

A woman who has FANTASTIC FLAUNT FLAIR, Oprah. Kudos Oprah for your generosity to your guests, staff and television audiences. You are a true School of Flaunt inspiration ... Our best wishes to you for continued success with the network, OWN!

And speaking of party inspirations, students, let your imagination go wild! Have a going away party but the persons who are going away are two of the guests (husband/wife or a couple). They will win your raffle gift, for a weekend getaway: e.g., New York City, New Orleans, San Francisco, Bermuda or the Bahamas. Just have a drawing at the beginning of the party, a limousine standing by to take the lucky couple to the airport. Then let the party begin for the happy losers. Consolations complete with a band, cocktails and sit down dinner. Presto! You have done it again! Another social coup for the season!

Are you thinking what can I do that is a little more intimate? Well this is a FLAUNT FLASH news-worthy idea. Host a caviar tasting party! You'll need toast points or blinis. Never us metal spoons only Mother of Pearl. Yes, some say for the "purist" no lemon, chopped egg whites or yolk and absolutely no finely chopped white onion or sour cream. We tend to disagree. Put it all out for everyone to partake of. You may offer a variety of Vodkas or dry champagne. From Trout Roe, Royal Farmed Siberian, Royal Transmontanus, Alverta President to Royal Ossetra, let your guests try them all. But here is the fun part, cover the labels. Let's see how fine your palette really is or are you the taste expert that you think you are?

An occasion like this should only be for your dearest friends who love caviar! Don't waste this on someone who still insists that they prefer a mixed salad followed by a good steak and a baked potato. Not that we can't enjoy this at a fine steak house like Ruth's Chris or Morton's but a tasting party for caviar aficionados should be for them and them only. For the perfect Caviar party, do please invite the founders of the School of Flaunt. Thank you and we promise not to divulge the caviar types!

****

Now we know that some of you have been invited to parties where cheap lingerie, plastic containers and gold fill jewelry are being sold.

We are begging you here, students, do not have one of these types of parties. They do not get the SOF seal of approval. Why would you ever invite your guests to your home with the expectation that they purchase something? Mind boggling that you would even consider such an occasion! We grimace at the very thought of having one of these much less attending! Total Flaunt Failure !

But the absolute worst are parties that sell sexual pleasuring devices, bring your gold jewelry and we'll have someone weigh it and write you a check or please come to get shot up with Botox supplied by a doctor from Mexico. These are all at the top of our list for Flaunt Failure No-Nos!

If you have had that one extra glass of champagne with your girl friends and think these would be fun, wait until you wake up the next day and then really think long and hard before you lower your standards. We've got news for you, this would get around town in a heart beat, even if it was a small group that attended. Enough said! We are going for the aspirin now from just talking about these sordid affairs.

**\*\*\*\***

Sixth, don't relegate invitations to the bottom of your list. Heaven forbid that we see you wandering through a party store trying to decide, should the invitation have balloons on it or just say, "You are invited." Pedestrian, students! As in dull, run of the mill and uninspired. Total Flaunt Flop.

Your invitations must always and we stress "always" be unique. Here are some ideas: they can range from a gorgeous personally hand written invitation on your custom stationary sent by snail mail, to an invitation again on your personal stationary accompanied by a single rose from your local florist. We'll let you put on your thinking caps here and come up with some great original ideas. Let us know what type of "Flaunt Fabulous" invitations you have sent out. And do we need to say this? Unfortunately we probably do, please don't ever send invitations by e-mail or twitter. Enough said because we do feel a slight sneer coming on our lips and do not want to go into a small snit on this topic.

****

Seventh, now we must talk about guest lists. Remember they are a mirror of your standards both socially and morally! Unfortunately several of the country's top executives have been indicted for fraud and misstatement of assets. Some have become quite infamous but please do not be tempted to invite these people to any social affairs. It can only lead to possible embarrassment for other guests or worse yet, people could assume you condone their activities. We draw the line at Martha. She was railroaded and we all know it. Besides, if you can get her to your table, you must be SOF material. We are not Flaunt Fawning here.

If you are inviting men, who have … shall we say, dabbled in inappropriate affairs leading them to make comments to the press about following their heart and soul mate, you are to leave them off of the guest list, until an appropriate time has passed, probably at least two years. Let's put it this way, until the divorce is final they are persona non grata. And never invite the two ex's to the same party! We repeat, NEVER, EVER, unless they had an amiable separation which probably in those high profile marriages is not going to be the case. There will always be a big time fight concerning the assets, e.g., who gets the baseball team, who is going to still live in the gorgeous penthouse and lastly who is going to keep which family pets. It can get very, very ugly and you don't want to be involved.

**Note**: Never "knowingly" invite someone's mistress to your party. Think about the gossip mill the next day or even worse the possibility of a cat fight where someone might end up in your pool, police having to be called or the paramedics. Wouldn't that be lovely splashed across the headlines of your local paper: Socialite's Party Ruined With Cat Fight Ending In Pool!

Now just when we thought we had seen it all, comes the famous White House PARTAY CRASHERS!! People, please, crashing any affair is bad form all around. One can have the hair, the makeup and outfit of the century, but if you were not invited, listen … DO NOT GO TO THE PARTY period. You will never be invited anywhere exhibiting this mega-level of bad manners! And may we remind you if you didn't even have the courtesy to do an RSVP, don't show up! You are definitely like the uninvited guest then. Think you will ever be invited back? The correct answer is NEVER!! And may we add here that one should never invite oneself. Example: At a large gathering a woman was overheard saying, "Are you having your party again to celebrate July 4th?" Nothing like putting the hostess on the spot! She dodged the question with a simple, "We're not sure." Sometimes being vague is the best way to handle rude people that are surfing for an invite!

And Puh-leese, we won't even go there on those terrible Facebook photos, which can be so dreadful, and get you removed quickly from the A list! Please refrain from using them. Enough said!

Lastly, as a guest in today's upper-crust society, you may arrive empty handed, but a quick "hand-written" thank you note should follow each event preferably with a small token of appreciation. A nice bottle of 1971 Dom Perignon, Ace of Spades or a bevy of flowers certainly won't hurt the hostess's feelings. Kion or Godiva chocolates are a nice touch, too. You "do" want to stay on the hosts "A" list and always be considered for that next party. Remember everyone does have their "A" list and "B" list. Your job is to make sure that you are so delightful, entertaining and witty that you will always be on the first list rather than the second. Second listers are usually people that the host and hostess are inviting strictly as a pay back, not because they really desire their company. Harsh but true, students.

****

All right, now that you have chosen a theme, made up your guest list, sent out your invitations and chosen a caterer for your affair, you have to set your table. In a quandary? No need. Just get out the Wedgwood china, Baccarat or Waterford crystal and some fine sterling. Of course there are many wonderful names in china and crystal and you can choose from an extensive list at your favorite china shop. Mixing it up is fun too and can make for a stunning table. You must be careful what the occasion is though. If it is Black Tie, sit down, then keep to the formal place settings.

## ALWAYS REMEMBER THIS: PRESENTATION IS EVERYTHING!

If you keep this advice in mind when planning your parties they will always be a success. Now read on please.

We hate to bring this up but some of you think that using paper or plastic plates, plastic utensils and plastic glasses for entertaining is acceptable. They are not and never will be! This would be considered the epitome of a Flaunt Flop for a party! The only place that you may use those items is for a pool party. No exceptions! Wine out of a plastic glass, puh-leese! The mere thought of having a fine wine out of a plastic glass is enough to make us apoplectic! Trust us that is something you never want to see! For those of you who don't know the term apoplectic, it means furious!

****

Now we will address the subject of "Being a House Guest!" Remember this rule, students: Fish and House Guests Smell After Three Days!

Heed this well. When you have been extended an invitation to another grand abode, please remember key House Guest Rules:

1. Always bring a Hostess/Host Gift. And it better be good. Substantial and Luxurious! See Colin Cowie's ideas of Hostess Gifts on his web site: www.colincowie.com. This gentleman can come to our homes anytime, so worthy are his gift selections!

2. Always take your Host/Hostess out for a meal … no leeches here, especially the Blood Sucking Money Leeches that drain one's host and hostess dry on out of the home entertainment. Pick up the TAB, students. Period.

3.  Let not the umbilical cord of life connect you to your Host/ Hostess! Think, plan and participate on your own or take into consideration that you offer to include your Host/ Hostess in said plans.

4.  Keep your Guest Room and Guest Bathroom in order ... do not make huge work for the staff. Treat the staff with respect and consideration! No whining and demands here. If you bring a personal maid or valet, make certain they are not being abused by any guest or local staff member. You will hear about this later, students! Believe you me!

5.  Do not overstay your welcome! Three days or less, period. Smell anything?

Here is some SOF advice. The problem of House Guests overstaying their welcome can be easily taken care of. How you ask? So simple, dear students. Purchase a vacation home on a few thousand acres. Think of a ranch, farm or plantation! Naturally it has its own airstrip. Fly them in for some fun, barbecues, horse back riding, shooting skeet, lounging at the pool. You get the idea. When you are tired of their company just have the staff pack their bags and tell them at lunch that the plane is waiting for them when they are finished. Smile and add, "Your bags are packed, no need to worry about them." Are you concerned that they will be insulted? Don't be! They will have had such a glorious time they will always want to come back for more. Remember you have been the consummate host and hostess. Just have a plan students, always a plan.

****

We might need to freshen up your views on hosting said House Guests! A true Host and Hostess leave nothing to chance! Here are a few pointers to live by when the invitations go out ...

1. Have enough room in the guest rooms and closet space for hanging. Not your guests, but their clothing.

2. Have enough staff to keep all under control with libations, food and towels, etc.

3. And this is a big one: Have enough FOOD. Nothing says wet blanket weekend as a hungry tummy! Guests poking about for nibs.

4. Arrange for games and entertainment, but allow one's guest to explore the village or area on their own if preferred. One should offer a car and driver, but we would hesitate on loaning your new Lamborghini.

5. Double check on pickup and delivery for the airport, train station, etc., … If you have your own air strip, so much the better.

6. Allow your guests to "Pick Up the Tab" when dining out. YOU do not have to do it all!

7. Wave them off with a FLAUNT FAREWELL and have a quiet Sunday evening after their departure. You should be proud, knowing that memories have been made. Follow up with a silver framed memento of your Flaunt Fun!

At this point we think it wise to bring up the question of house staff that is so necessary for fine entertaining, if not just managing your home. We do not refer to our staff as "the hired help." These are finely trained people that hopefully live for your next command! Treat them fairly and politely. Always pay well and you can then enjoy their loyalty and your life to the fullest.

SOF recommends the following: Head butler who can double as a valet, your chauffeur in uniform, a fine chef (remember to be discriminating here), a nurse or nanny, who is preferably English, maid or maids, gardeners, stable help, social secretary and personal body guard. A background check should be done on one and all even if they come highly recommended. They also need to sign a confidentiality agreement. That is mandatory, no ifs, ands, or buts, for being hired. Whew … so much is needed, students.

We would like to add a little more detail on the question of a nanny for your little ones because we know how important this issue will be. We recommend an English nanny. Preferably they have been trained at the Norland College in England. Norland requires they study for two years. Their graduates are not only proficient at potty training and catering children's parties, but have even completed an internship in the maternity ward. Remember a nanny is hired strictly for child care and not for domestic labor. You will need maids for that. Get ready to pay as much as $500 a week plus benefits, and paid vacations for that Norland graduate. Another Beatrix Potter Moment!

One last "very" important thought, students, please do not "steal" others' staff! Especially chefs and nannies!! It is just BAD form all around. Not to mention once you have stolen staff from another family, your name will be MUD around town. Be Forewarned! This is high Flaunt Failure. Remember, if they can be stolen then you really don't want them working for you. Just like a cheating husband, they will cheat with a new employer again and leave you in the lurch! Plus, you having stolen staff will become common knowledge and trust us the social invitations will CEASE! Was it worth it? Never! Remember the "A" list.

****

Continuing with entertaining brings us to Children's Affairs:

When it comes to "one-upmanship," kids party planning is off the charts!! Let's be reasonable, students, 40 grand for little Madison's 5th is a bit much! Are we just having these for our egos? Answer: probably yes. The facts simply are that a child under seven in our humble opinion is not going to really remember an event of this magnitude. So stick with a small family affair, with close school friends and no school bullies present. Example: The Duke of Gloucester held a sit down luncheon for his 6 year old daughter and their nannies were standing behind each child to help with the cutting and serving for their charge. Parents were in the large drawing room sipping champagne! Oh those Brits, that is a tad stuffy.

So let's think of something fun. We do like the games, bouncy things, ponies, cotton candy machines, etc., … but have your liability insurance up to date! Remember the birthday cakes today sometimes are as grandiose as a wedding cake. Will the little ones be excited about a wedding cake look? We doubt it. So put together a massive cupcake cake or something that carries off your birthday party theme and all of the children will be squealing with joy. Send them home with some fun remembrances in a cute bag and voila a great day! Lastly, if money is no object go ahead and hire the Wiggles to entertain. We know the little ones really enjoy them! Sorry over the top on that recommendation but it would be fun for them, n'est-ce pas?

# Lesson Five Quiz

1. When giving a party what is most important?
    a. Displayed plastic containers, plastic plates, plastic glasses
    b. One-upmanship
    c. Caterer
    d. Invitations
    e. b, c, d

ANSWER: E – Didn't we say you would make us apoplectic if you used PLASTIC for entertaining!!!! That is not a good idea students to make your teachers really upset with you. You could be asked to leave the School of Flaunt.

2. What should you never serve at a "sit down," black tie dinner?
    a. Meatloaf and muscatel in a simple brown paper bag
    b. Chipped beef on toast points
    c. Beluga caviar, Duck a l'orange, Ace of Spades, Grand Marnier Soufflé and port with cheeses
    d. A & B

ANSWER: D

3. Cheese is like fine wine. What should you never serve with your Sandman 1970 port?
    a. Processed wine and cheese swirled spread
    b. Jalapeno flavored cheese in a can
    c. Triple Cream Brie, English Blue Stilton, Aged Cheddar
    d. A&B
    e. None of the above

ANSWER: D – Remember we said, Never!

4. If guests arrive one hour early for dinner what should a SOF devotee do?
   a. Have them help out in the kitchen or park cars
   b. Tell them you are so glad they are the first to arrive!
   c. Ask them to run the vacuum, one last time
   d. A&C
   e. None of the above

ANSWER: B

5. List five party themes with invitations and menus in 60 seconds!

HURRY UP, STUDENTS, OR YOU HAVE TO REREAD THIS LESSON.

6. List two personal friends you would seat next to the following:
   Your US Senator
   A Chairman of the Board from a Fortune 500 Company
   Your spouse
   Bernie Madoff **

   **Madoff isn't going anywhere … that was a TRICK Question, students! Just checking that you are up on current New York and Palm Beach events!

   If you don't have two best friends that you could seat next to any of the above burn your address book and start making some new friends!

7. Who should never be on your invitation list?
   a. An indicted CEO or CFO
   b. A mud wrestler

    c. A known narcotics dealer
    d. Any of the above

ANSWER: D – Please would you even consider having these people to your home?

8. What does the term "In your cups" mean?
    a. Seeking a brand of china
    b. Reading tea leaves
    c. Drunk and slurring your words
    d. Too much sugar

ANSWER: C – For extra credit, how do you politely remove that intoxicated person from the party? You must be able to answer this or you will never be a SOF hostess or host. If you are having problems answering this please contact us at www.schoolofflaunt.com

9. When planning Children's Parties, what details are extremely necessary?
    a. No Bullies
    b. Ponies, Jumpy Things, Cake
    c. Entertainment such as: Clown, Balloon Maker, Juggler etc., . . .
    d. Liability Insurance Rider
    e. Protection for the Clown from nasty children
    f. All of the above

ANSWER: F

10. What is Petrossian?
    a. Restaurant
    b. Caviar Importer
    c. Total decadence

d. A great place to buy a hostess gift
e. All of the above

ANSWER: E – This is why you always have to be doing your research students. If in NYC and you need a caviar fix it is the only place to go!! **Flaunt Flash News**: There is now another Petrossian in West Hollywood. For those of you in other parts of the country they will ship. Thank you, there is a SOF God.

11. How do you handle your staff when you are angry?
    a. Throw a cell phone at them
    b. Cut their pay for the day
    c. Fire them and then hire them back
    d. Use your Taser on them
    e. Go to a private space and cool down!

ANSWER: E – Do you want to end up on the front of the Tabloids for acting like a TOTAL PIG?

12. When is it appropriate to attend an event without an Invitation?

ANSWER: NEVER!!! HAVE YOU NOT LEARNED ANYTHING? GO BACK AND READ LESSON 5 COMPLETELY THREE TIMES. YOU ARE A FLAUNT FAILURE.

13. When is it appropriate to call the "authorities" and report your party
    crashing wife missing?

ANSWER: Probably never...we couldn't resist.

# LESSON SIX:
## SOF Attitude, Manners and Etiquette ...
### "Are You Behaving Badly"

IN OUR INTRODUCTION we spoke about how all of you were starting to resemble actors in fast food commercials. Unfortunately our society seems to be revolving around the mundane and reality television. Do you think that behaving badly, which brings some notoriety and fame for a few weeks, is a primer for how to lead your life? Please, students, stop and think, these people are famous for being so "depressingly ordinary." We ask you to look into the mirror for we now need to address behaving badly. This might sound harsh but unfortunately it is true today! Now please read on, students.

1.  Correct manners and polished attitude will be your ticket for entrance into the finest homes and boardrooms. Here are some definite musts for SOF devotees to use, learn and practice.
    We quote famed author, Meg Cabot:

    "Be approachable and kind. You are lucky and you know that. Think how the poor folks feel? Never be above it all in thought, actions and demeanor."

2.  Always say "please." Your lives are so finely tuned by your staff, that you may think this word is no longer necessary, but as with

"excuse me," stellar manners separate the cream from the curd, students!

Example: Recently we were dining at a fine restaurant and mentioned to the waiter how much we had previously enjoyed the squash medley that had been served as a seasonal vegetable. The waiter apologized and said that the chef had not prepared it that night. In passing the waiter made a comment that the chef was serving pureed butternut squash with the scallops. We sighed and said, "Oh, I'm sure it must be delicious but we had decided on beef tonight. But we will dream about that wonderful squash. It was truly superb. <u>Please</u> let the chef know how much we enjoyed it." Well, guess what, students? A gravy boat of pureed squash appeared with our dinner entrees (No extra charge on the bill). It was absolutely delicious and it was all because we were polite, used flattery and that special word PLEASE. Do not confuse this with puh-leese. Puh-leese is used in those situations where you are expressing disdain.

Also, remember when you are asking the wait staff for something you should always say. "Please when you have an opportunity may I have ' ......... ' " When they bring said item, one should always say, "Thank you." Even if you have to stop your conversation. It takes how long to say thank you, students? You can always pick up where you left off in the conversation.

Since we are discussing restaurants can you answer this? How do you signal the waiter that you are ready to order? O.K., we are waiting … We haven't heard your answer. For those of you who answered, close your menu, you just got extra credit and go to the head of the class! You have made us proud.

And one last thing for restaurant etiquette. DON'T TALK ON YOUR CELL PHONE, DON'T TEXT AND DON'T TWEET. Have we made ourselves perfectly clear? Your answer now should be, Yes.

3.  One's voice is of critical import. It should be modulated at all times. Shrieking and swearing are only for the tacky. Now, try this trick: extend your lower jaw and speak. Like it? OH YOU STUPID IDIOT! No one speaks this way. At least no one with any brains! So what to do? We would recommend that you listen to your voice on a recorder. Do you sound too nasal, regional or high pitched as in resembling a 5 year old child who just answered the phone? Then it is time to get yourself to a voice coach.

A few simple lessons, practice sessions and you will have the enunciation and vocals of a Prime Time Evening News commentator. People will pay attention to what you have to say because delivery is half the battle. The other is substance. We can only help you so much, you will have to work on the substance issue yourself. One last thought about accents and we mean no disrespect but there are a few accents from the East Coast and we will not go into which ones but drop them now! Oh never mind, drop the Jersey accent, do you want to be confused with the Jersey Shore TV crowd and talk about no substance either. You get the point, students.

Just one other little suggestion that can make a real difference. What you ask? It is about using a recorder. If you would like to show your children how poor their language skills are just record them having a conversation and then play it back to them. Does this sound familiar? Like … amazing … uhh … like … amazing … uhh. "Like" can I kill myself now if I have to listen to another teenager!

And we are not letting you off the hook either. Never use these slang expressions in a meeting or the board room: dope, dude, sweet, amazing, or the totally overdone Booyah! Why? Because, Dude, you will be off of the Board pronto!! Booyah! Understand? Asked to leave any board, well eyebrows will be raised to say the least. Social Invitations will be lost …

Lastly, there is the proverbial "HUH." The height of rudeness to use when you don't hear someone. Repeat after us, "I'm sorry I didn't hear you." "Pardon me" which can be used in other situations, too, or "Please" as they say in Cincinnati. Maybe not use that one unless you are in Cincinnati, seems to confuse the non-natives.

Now here is a major important School of Flaunt phrase to memorize. This one will get you out of most any situation: "Darrhhling I would love to help you but I simply can't." Start using it today and you will find that it works perfectly. You have the pesky neighbor always bothering you, use it. The Committee chair calls you to do grunt work for her, use it. Panhandlers bothering you on the street, use it. What can anyone say back to that remark? You have told them that you would love to help them but you simply can't. Bye-bye!

4.  We stand firm on good posture. An erect head and nose angle of 45 degrees will have you looking like a freak and a snob! So be very careful here, shoulders back, head erect, nose in a forward position and pleasant facial expression at all times. Don't look sappy; this is a fine line, students.

    Ladies, start practicing by walking with a book on your head. If you have small daughters now is the time to get them to practice with you and then their posture will never be an issue. It must become instinctual. As natural as breathing in and breathing out. When your Grandmother was practicing walking with a book on top of her head it was for a purpose. To be able to glide in and out of a room.

    God forbid that someone describe you as "looking like John Wayne or Clint Eastwood" striding across the street unless you are a man! This brings us to gait, ladies. Don't walk like you are in a five mile race nor should you walk like your are on your tip-toes. Don those four inch pair of high heels and place a book on your head, now start walking. We promise you that it will all fall into place. Lady Gaga could have used that advice when she took a tumble on those ghastly ugly platform shoes that were probably at least 5 inches high.

Last of all, remember to tuck that buttock down, put your shoulders back, pretend that you have a string coming out of the top of your head that someone is pulling on, hold your head up high and throw that gorgeous cape over your shoulder. Now you've got it! Notice we did not say, "Now you've got it, babe." Drop the babe comment from any of your expressions.

And before we forget, ladies, please know how to sit in a chair. If you have ever seen Ivanka Trump sitting, she is the perfect example of how it is done! Sit erect, not slouched, do not cross your legs at the knees but at your ankles. Lightly rest your folded hands in your lap. Sounds stilted to you? If you saw Ivanka you would say, "the epitome of a lady."

5. How to enter the room? Remember if you have style, you will enter, stop for a moment, slightly pause in a model's pose, smile ever so graciously, make eye contact with someone in the room and then glide over to them like they are the most special person there. Greet them with either, "it is so wonderful to see you again" or if you haven't met them before stop, smile and simply say, "I haven't had the pleasure of meeting you. My name is ...... "

Cate was once at a Benefit Gala. She spotted an older woman who looked not only wonderful but surely like someone that she thought would be interesting, too. As they made eye contact she glided across the room and said, "I think we might have met previously." To which the older Grand Dame replied with a smile, "I'm not sure but you certainly look like someone I would like to know." Now if that is not SOF talk then nothing is! A few minutes of an interesting conversation started an instant friendship. Take our advice, students, again it is the small things that open doors for you but you need to be ready when the opportune time arrives. This short conversation lead to invitations to parties, polo matches and meeting other interesting individuals.

Trust us, others will be watching you even if only from the corner of their eye and they too will want to speak with you. Remember, SOF devotees, it is all about your image and self confidence. Soon it will be totally natural and you will not even know you are doing it. This is your goal. Think we don't know what we are talking about? Well trust us, a big name star who will remain nameless here even makes herself stop ever so slightly when entering the first class cabin of an airline. Statements, students, you are making one! It is a way of announcing that the party can now really begin because you have arrived.

Lastly, do not monopolize the time of any VIP at an event. Others want to speak with them, too. And you, too, need to be working the room. People want to feel important and that is what you should be doing. Remember, people love to talk about themselves. They will leave the conversation and party thinking you are wonderful just because they had such a good time talking about themselves. Works every time, trust us. Just throw out those little tidbits of information that are appropriate and let them run with it. Smile, laugh and "tear up" at the correct time! Aren't you the conversationalist!

6.  Now to settle the dispute between "cool and cold stares." Cool is for looking around seeking out friends in a restaurant or reviewing the latest fashions in Milano. Cold is for making one's point in a hostile takeover board room. Not suitable for real life please. Probably best to practice this at home in the mirror. We, at the School of Flaunt, think that Ivanka Trump Kushner has this down perfectly.

7.  Always look well-heeled. Well-heeled, adj., meaning plentifully supplied with money as in looking polished, prosperous, as in

affluent. You want people to say in their heads, "now she/he looks like they've got the bucks."

**Flaunt Flash Story**: We were recently at one of the more prestigious race tracks in the country. No it was not for Opening Day but our foursome had on the required outfits for that. Picture ladies in hats, Lapis earrings to match the color in a dress, gentlemen in their linen sport jackets and NO jeans but wearing a good pair of Hickey Freeman slacks. You get the picture. As the foursome approached security, the security guard took one look and just ushered them through. Who says that if you look the part it doesn't hurt! Obviously, students, this won't work with the TSA at the airport if the detector goes off but normally they are not going to randomly pull you out of line for an extra body scan. Just a thought.

We hesitate to mention these final points, but they must be said:

8.  A FLAUNT FIRM handshake. No limp wimps from the women and no bone crushers from the men. There is nothing worse than feeling like you just shook hands with a dead fish or that you have to shake off the pain. This is especially important for women and men in the work place when they shake hands!

9.  Stand tall. In fact, be tall if at all possible. We don't recommend lifts for men in their shoes. Sorry, fellows, if you were not blessed with height, then you simply have to marry a tall woman. Hopefully some of her genes will be passed on to the next generation. We also feel that it is necessary to bring up the "short man syndrome." Please, gentlemen, if physical height was not one of your God-given assets, then don't try to make up for it by that over-the-top, macho attitude or acting like the little Hitler at work. Just be yourself, hopefully that is sophisticated, urbane and witty! And for you ladies, get out the 4 inch heels and hopefully you can be eye to eye with some of those Vogue models.

10. Control your pinkies, people!! Yes, we have seen you sticking those short end digits up while drinking from your bone china and Starbucks cups. Try to control yourself, you look idiotic!

11. Know your table manners! Get those elbows off of the table! How many times do we have to tell you that you are not in a fast food restaurant? Gobbling your food and using your silverware like shovels is forbidden. Knowing how a table is to be set sounds so "old school" but how do you think it will look if you are invited to the White House for a state dinner and you have no idea which fork to use. When you finish a course do you know where your knife and fork are to be placed and how? "Course" that means appetizer, soup, salad, entree or dessert, students. Do know there is a reason you place your utensils in the center, on the right hand side of your plate, when you are finished. It is a signal to the waiter that he or she may take your plate. On which side will they serve you? The left students, because if they are clearing it will be on the right! This way you always know where the wait staff will be. Remember this little diddy, "Serve from the left, clear from the right, stand up, sit down, Fight, Fight, Fight." Who said you couldn't learn anything from your days as a pledge in a sorority or fraternity?

    We hate to HAVE to mention this again but under no circumstances crash a party at the White House … you will be finished in society. So you might end up on another one of those Housewives of D.C. television episodes but is that how you want to be remembered? We hope not.

12. What do you do with your napkin? Don't tuck it into your shirt, gentlemen, put it in your lap! The only napkin that should be tucked into your collar or tied around your neck is a lobster bib. Very important, when you are going to leave the table but are returning, the napkin should be left on the seat of your chair not on the table. Why? You are telling the waiter that you plan on returning to finish your meal, don't remove my plate. You should

return to find the napkin placed on the back of your chair neatly folded. Obviously we are not talking Applebee's here but a true SOF restaurant for a gastronome. But the same rule applies even at non-SOF establishments, leave your napkin on the seat not on the table. Oh my God, students, please if you were never given any at home training for good table manners or manners period, please go to an etiquette school or at the very least get a book on manners and start reading immediately. No manners or lack of them is the first sign that you are not SOF material.

**Flaunt Flash Failure:** Cat fights, tipping over tables and ripping out another's hair extensions are never acceptable. Period.

13. Another small point here, under no circumstances, gentlemen, should you ever "not" open the car door for a lady. If there is valet parking or you are being chauffeured then don't worry about this point. And speaking of doors (not revolving ones) please, gentlemen, always open the door for a lady and then hold it open for her to pass through. And ladies, if a gentleman does do this for you smile and say thank you. Appreciate civil manners and reciprocate!

14. Always carry a handkerchief. At the very least some tissues. Never blow your nose in public unless it is an emergency. Excuse yourself and go to preferably an empty room or the loo (French for bathroom) to blow your nose. NEVER AND WE REPEAT HERE, NEVER use your napkin as a handkerchief in a restaurant. It is for your lap not your nose, students.

This is a true story and is the epitome of poor manners and absolutely no class. As you might remember Alexandra was a flight attendant. She preferred to work international flights, in first class, since the flight attendants who worked "up front" had the first dibs on the left over Beluga Caviar, but then we digress. One flight she was walking down the aisle and saw a man in first class, no less, that actually had his finger in his nose. No not just touching the end of his nose but digging to China! Oh yes it is true, we do not make up these stories. But the worst part is that he rolled up the "stuff" that came out of his nose on the end of his finger and then flipped it into the air. You gasp; we repeat again, it is true! Trust us the entire crew knew about it and they all washed their hands in Vodka when they had to touch anything he had touched! Heaven only knows where his hands had been during the rest of the flight and we would take bets that he probably didn't bother to wash them in the lavatory, either. First class, "No!" Manners, "No!" Couth, "No!" Yes, he was only fit for a jail cell! We actually feel sorry for his cell partner.

Since we are on this topic we might as well go further. Why do men feel that they can blow their nose on a golf course by holding one finger on a nostril and then blowing? We understand that this is referred to as a "snot rocket." We are feeling slightly overcome and faint at this picture! Does anyone have a fan?

We will not repeat this, take a handkerchief or tissue with you before you jump in that golf cart. You may be able to get away with this when you are in the boonies of Mississippi, or Montana duck hunting, or ice fishing in Wisconsin, but not on a golf course! Enough said, we will now continue with something that is a little more genteel.

15. If at all possible learn a few words of French. We have included a few French terms to use in your everyday lives. French is also important to know for ordering from the menu in a fine restaurant. Remember, SOF gentlemen, it is very nice to be able to order for your significant other. Speaking to the waiter, "the lady will have … " Aren't you the debonair romantic who also knows his French. Next thing we know you will be throwing your coat over a mud puddle for her.

So with some practice and memorization of our SOF pointers we think that you can go out now for a fine dining experience. We would like to suggest some excellent restaurants but, alas, they change frequently and if the chef should decide to leave and start his own place then everything is up for grabs. SOF would like to take a moment and bless these chefs, though, for their discriminating and innovative menus! We bow to your greatness! In closing just remember great restaurants are always being added to the "A" list and unfortunately some are deleted. This is very important: always keep up with the latest and greatest. If for no other reason than for some good flaunt conversation.

Lastly, don't forget you can also find some great diners and places off the beaten track that you should try. Yes we know, we said diners and we will go so far as to say dumps, too, but there are little slices of gastronomic greatest to be found everywhere. No need to dress up, jeans and flip-flops are totally acceptable there. Best part is the price is right and you can take out the entire family for the same price as one dinner at a 4 Star restaurant. Remember finding a new FLAUNT FISCAL place to dine can be fun for you and your friends. Then start spreading the news about your new eateries. Always be a trend setter! People love to hear about a new deal!

**Flaunt Fiscal Tip**: Groupon anyone?

As we said earlier, nothing polishes one more than a few well placed French phrases! Interject the following into your everyday conversation and watch out! People will treat you with more respect and the doors will open!

Au Pair: Children's nanny that comes from another country
Gaucherie: Faux pas, tactlessness
Je ne sais quoi: I know not what
Maison de campagne: Country house
Maison de passe: Brothel
Maisonette: Small house
Maison de ville: Town house
Haute Couture: High fashion

Haute Cuisine: High-end cooking
Merci beaucoup: Thank you very much
Mesalliance: Unsuitable union; marriage of inferior social position
Grandeur: The quality of being grand. (Noble)
Gauche: Clumsy, socially awkward, Tacky!
Bon Voyage: Good voyage as in a "trip"
Bon Chance: Good luck
Noblisse Oblige: Nobility obliges with good behavior
N'est-ce pas?: Is it not?
Panache: Spirited self confidence
Objet d'art: Small objects of artistic value
Respondez Si Vous Plait: Respond if you please … RSVP *

*Always let your hostess know if you will be attending with a written reply or phone call.

**\*\*\*\***

We have only grazed the surface with manners but we feel so strongly about them since they make life so much easier for all that we would like to recommend the following for reference material:

John Molloy's, *Dress for Success, Live for Success*
Amy Vanderbilt's, *Book of Etiquette*
Charlotte Ford's, *Book of Modern Manners*

## Lesson Six Quiz

For Lesson Six we will deviate from Questions to exercises to be performed.

1. Voice modulation. Extend lower jaw and corners of your mouth and repeat six times. TACKY, TACKY, TACKY.

STOP! This was a trick exercise. Never speak this way and remove anyone from your Board and/or guest list who does!

2. Practice the Cold stare for Hostile Takeovers, Death Threats, Violent Paparazzi, etc., … then the Cool stare for looking around a restaurant and lastly your approachable look. Please practice these three times a day!

3. Reverting to the tried but true, please place a book on the top of your head and walk in your home or office for 20 minutes a day. Careful not to let Hostile Takeover types see this.

4. Shake hands firmly with five persons a day. For example: the door-man, grocer, sales clerks, if appropriate. Remember, never be a wimp! But don't do any bone crushers either! Bring hand sanitizer just to be safe. H1N1, doncha know.

5. For one week make a conscious effort every time you pick up a coffee cup to extend your little finger.

STOP! REVIEW THIS LESSON, THIS IS AN OUTDATED PRACTICE!! WE NOW KEEP OUR PINKIES CLOSED, PEOPLE.

6. Memorize for conversations and also learn how to spell all French phrases mentioned in Lesson Six.

   Now grade yourself, if you have less than 90% correct you must repeat and test yourself until you can get that passing grade. Merci beaucoup.

7. For extra credit repeat this phrase until it becomes effortless:

   "Darling I would love to help you, but I simply can't." Heed our words, students, this simple phrase will get you out of many a predicament. Think about it!

8. Repeat: dope, dude, like … like, uh, amazing, like awesome, Booyah and now you know what I'm talkin' about. If these sound like familiar banter then put your baseball cap on backwards or sideways. Now we ask you to look in the mirror. If you think that you are Boardroom material please dispose of our book and tell no one that you have ever read it!

9. Borderline phrases: Sweet, fresh and tasty should only apply to food groups not experiences … enough said.

10. Please note that the well-heeled always speak in plurality. Practice saying: "Let's go for a walk in the gardens, Shall we go to the stables, Cocktails anyone?" If you can make it plural do it!

(This page intentionally left blank)

## LESSON SEVEN:
## Vacations: Location, Location, Location!
### "The Value of the Thread Count"

WHERE ON EARTH could you possibly go for a vacation? Is your passport up to date? Bought your new Tumi or Louis Vuitton luggage? Then the answer is any place you choose! But please remember there are always those few resort areas that are the gold standard you should consider using for comparison. To suggest a few, Monte Carlo or Lake Como for the "people watching," a secluded resort in Hawaii, for back to enchantment, Fiji for total relaxation, or best yet, your own private island! We also found a wonderful hideaway in the British Virgin Islands for the active and inactive alike! The Bitter End Yacht Club has long been the private retreat of the well-heeled. So break out your topsiders and learn to sail, snorkel, and scuba or just admire the unsurpassed beauty of this glorious resort in Virgin Gorda. Your neighbor will be Sir Richard Branson on his private island, Necker, and that's not too bad either.

Now speaking of Necker Island, we are sure that most of you must know that it is owned by Sir Richard Branson owner of Virgin Airlines. Well, Students of Flaunt, if you have made it big such as Oprah, numerous movie stars, rock stars or born into royalty and need the ultimate private getaway then this island is for you.

You can rent the entire island for a mere $47,000 per day but you can also have twenty eight of your favorite friends or relatives stay with you as your guests, too. Do the math, students, approximately $1700 per day, per guest for a private island. We are sure that doesn't include food or beverages though! But think cliff side villas and pool, exploring those private beaches or sipping the bubbly while overlooking the Caribbean. Don't want the children or relatives there then rent it for you and your significant other. Trés chic!

**Flaunt Flash News**: We were sad to learn of the fire which destroyed the main house on the island. We are certain that Sir Richard will rebuild a Flaunt Fabulous home from the ashes!

Oh, so now we have wet your appetite for island vacations. Think Bonefish in the Bahamas. You may purchase a stay there for 50,000 Euros ($71,000 +/-U.S.) per week for the entire island which guarantees total privacy or bring up to 14 of your personal friends. Seems outrageous. Do the math. That is only $700 per day for each guest if you bring 14.

Don't like that idea then fly over to Spain to the Isla de sa Ferradura located just off of Ibiza. You won't believe what this island has to offer. It has a "flaunt fabulous" hacienda with a separate cave complex that has a whirlpool, Turkish bath, sauna, and a beauty salon with massage facilities. Yes, a separate cave complex! Oh meet your caveman there!

Add a little water-skiing, jet-skiing, fishing and surfing and you will be ready for that feather bed! We feel confident that if you want that, they will make sure you can have it! All of this for a mere 147,000 Euros ($209,000 +/- U.S.) for a week on this spectacular island and they can accommodate 12 of your guests. It is all about the Flaunt, students. We will be happy to join you as your guests, too! If you cannot afford this resort, simply log on to their website for some good dancing music!

http://www.islaferradura.com

We can see Dancing With the Stars in your future!

**Flaunt Fiscal Tip**: O.K., we hear you. Something more reasonable. Go to the Forsyth Island in New Zealand. A helicopter ride from New Zealand's capital, Wellington, and you will find 2100 acres, with 20 miles of ocean frontage and 30 miles of walking and hiking trails. There is a wharf, farmhouse and sheep-shearing quarters for you to explore. All of this from 1,000 Euro per day for the entire island. They will also allow you to bring eight guests. Now that is a deal! $170 per day per guest. You and the sheep, "quaint" but you did ask for something more reasonable. Take some Sauvignon Blanc on the helicopter to drink on your stay and enjoy the hiking and beaches.

****

Students, you must always remember this: a SOF vacation is "not" just a hotel room, or villa, but is an experience. One to always be able to bring up later when sunning, skiing or spending across the globe! It is so nice to be able to reminisce with friends and new acquaintances over cocktails or tea about that wonderful new hideaway you found. So clever and interesting you will be, students!

How to get their attention? These are experiences that should make them listen! How would you like to spend three nights in the Ice Hotel in Sweden? Yes, you will stay in a hotel made out of ice. Ice art and sculptures will surround you while you sleep in a thermal sleeping bag on a "special" bed of ice and snow, on reindeer skins. We have no idea what a special bed of ice and snow is? But, thank God, when you awake in the morning there is cup of hot lingonberry juice at your bedside.

Now to be perfectly honest we at the School of Flaunt consider that one step from camping in the Arctic, in the summer time, to see migrating Moose. Puh-leese, do you realize that you will have twenty four hours of sunshine in the summer when you are doing this? Both of these trips sound like nightmares to us, either too cold or too much sun but you might be in for adventures? Please don't invite Alexandra or Cate.

What else is very unique? Try going to the Serrin House Boutique "Cave" Hotel in Cappadonia, Turkey. Yes, students, we do not kid you here. Architects and designers have used cutting edge design to make up five guest rooms replete with fine cotton linens and custom made toiletries. We at the School of Flaunt would need more than toiletries to get us to stay inside cave rooms, but here again, this is personal taste and it certainly is something to talk about over cocktails. We have the perfect idea; you stay there and get back to us. Then maybe we will try cave dwelling?

****

Now, we prefer when traveling to major cities for business or sightseeing that you should only stay at hotels that were meant for Kings and Queens. You are not looking for a bed and board arrangement, that so many hotel chains are just one step above, but a "hand and foot" establishment. In other words, the staff is there to wait on you "hand and foot!" Example: In the finer hotels in Hong Kong, room service is so fast that if you are spending that extra ten minutes in bed beware. You better have your robe at the ready, that of course the hotel has supplied for you, because each floor has its own staff to immediately take care of your needs. None of this waiting 45 minutes to get a pot of coffee. A full breakfast will be at your door in 15 minutes or less!

Here is a list of some of the finest accommodations in major cities around the world which can be described as a "Study in Luxury." Known for their serene comfort and exemplary services, SOF salutes the following hotels for their continuing "Top Drawer" service for the upper-crust. These hotels are listed in alphabetical order and not necessarily in order of preference:

Bangkok:
    Oriental
Boston:
    Eliot
Canada:
    Sea Lion Pointe
    Sonora Resort

Chicago:
  Ritz Carlton
  The Four Seasons
  Trump Hotel
  Peninsula
Dubai:
  The Burj Al Arab, 7 Star
Hawaii:
  Halekulani, Oahu
  Mauna Kai, Hawaii
  Ritz Carlton, Maui
  Four Seasons, Maui
Hong Kong:
  The Mandarin
  The Peninsula
  Island Shangri-La
London:
  Claridges
  Loundes Hotel
  Savoy
  The Goring (Where Kate Middleton's family stayed for the royal
  wedding!)
Mexico:
  The Hacienda, Xcanatun
  Esperanza, An Auberge Resort, Los Cabos
Munich:
  Hotel Vier Jahreszeiter
New York:
  The Four Seasons
  The Pierre Hotel
  Plaza Athenee
  St. Regis
  Peninsula
Paris:
  George V

Plaza Athenee
The Ritz
San Francisco:
Four Seasons
Ritz Carlton
Mandarin Oriental
Singapore:
Shangri-La
Toronto:
Four Seasons
Vienna:
Hotel Imperial
Washington, DC:
Four Seasons Georgetown
Four Seasons Washington, DC
Zurich:
Baur Au Lac

One small note SOF devotees: Please do "take tea" when you are staying in these poshest of hotels. Many varieties of herbal, fruity, Earl
Grey or English Breakfast and scads of scones! Don't forget the water-
cress sandwiches, sans crust and there you have it, a scene in which
Noel Coward would feel at home! Lastly, remember pinkies in place,
students, and no rowdy or raucous behavior, please. We do have our
standards.

****

Ah, now we can hear you saying but I do love to stay in those boutique hotels. Whether for vacations or business these gems sparkle all
of the time. Planning a trip to Scotland? Ever hear of the Allandale
Wilderness Reserve? Set among gorgeous natural beauty in the high-
lands, this remote estate will provide you with all of the amenities
and more. Or perhaps a trip to Monte Carlo? Well take a little side
trip to Cap Este, Eze-Bord-de-mer in France. A mansion on a 5 acre

private peninsula surrounded by the Mediterranean sea, hosts many a SOF devotee. Then there is one of our favorites, the Draycott Hotel in London. 5 Star with only 35 perfectly appointed rooms or suites. Edwardian splendor at its best! Start researching today for that new jewel of a hotel. Happy sleeping on those 650 thread count sheets, students. Sweet dreams!

****

Earlier we mentioned that vacations are a wonderful way to reminisce and to share stories with friends. They can be great shopping excursions and learning experiences, too. What could be more fun than wandering the world in pursuit of the best wines? Just starting in the United States we have some of the world's best in Napa and Sonoma, California, and then there is the Willamette Valley in Oregon.

The Auberge Du Soleil in Napa has wonderful accommodations with apartment size rooms and a truly wonderful restaurant with spectacular views. You can become a vacationing epicure and note this, most restaurants will allow you to bring your own wine. Of course, there is a modest corkage fee but we have also found that some restaurants do not charge if your bottle is over five years old or you have dropped the big bucks for caviar as an appetizer. Ask when you make your dinner reservations if they have a corkage fee.

So, now you are a true SOF pilgrim, traveling the world, motivated by love of fine wine and food, therefore you must start your quest for the best. A trip to an ancient wine region in Rioja, Spain, should be on your list. For Flaunt Foodies dine like the locals. Start with some delicious tapas and do try Piquillo peppers stuffed with cheese. For a main course think, roasted Lamb which is a local favorite or Venison with a plum sauce. All can be enjoyed with a divine "big" Rioja red. Our mouths are watering now! Oh, stop with the talk about your cholesterol count! You aren't going to eat like this all of the time! And lastly, this is a fabulous spot that is not overrun with tourists. Do your research and visit this little known area of the world to miss the camera jockeys who have five little ones in tow.

From there you can fly over to Italy and then go straight to Tuscany. You should become familiar with some outstanding Sangiovese to Chianti. Take the A1 highway and visit Chuisi, Siena, Arezzo and Firenze. Now forget the spaghetti with tomato sauce for we aren't talking Spaghetti O's here! Think of Crostini con Salsiccia (sausage) followed by a Ribollita soup and then some Florentine Roast Pork. For dessert there is always the classic Tiramisu but if they have Frittelle Di Riso (fried rice fritters) on the menu try them. We don't think you will be disappointed. Of course when in Italy do have an Expresso. Heaven, you're in SOF food heaven! Buon Appetito!

A small point here: adults and children drink cappuccino in the morning. In the evening adults all drink espresso. Try not to look like a tourist! And don't order tea, you aren't in Kansas or London now, Dorothy. Your waiter will look at you like you are an alien from another planet. Oh and one more thought, if you are driving in Italy, stop signs in the countryside are "merely a suggestion." That is a direct quote from one of our Italian friends. Do slow down, look in either direction but don't stop. You might get rear ended. You in a neck brace, sipping wine, not a pretty picture.

So you've never been to South America, well your wine pilgrimage can now take you to Santiago, Chile. You are going to see the Andes mountains! They are breathtaking, students, and remember to have good camera equipment with you. But back to your wine pilgrimage, it is recommended that you hire a driver and do make an appointment with the wineries. You will be greeted like a Flaunt Favorite guest, which is as it should be, and you will also taste with the winemakers/owners in a private setting. Oh, making new Flaunt Friendships is so rewarding! As for dining, be adventuresome. Try sauteed Baby Octupus with pisco sour mayonnaise or Rabbit dumplings with mango ginger chutney. Enjoy a Sauvignon Blanc, Pinot Noir or a Merlot and Cabernet blend. Then jet over for a few days to either Argentina or Brazil. You will be surprised at all of the sights to see and fine dining experiences you will have there, too.

Now you can zip off to Steelenbosch, South Africa. Where? Less than an hour's drive from Cape Town, you will find Stellenbosch Sauvignons and Bordeaux reds. We promise you will not be disappointed in these wines! As for dining, get ready for South African "braai" meaning barbeque. They will barbeque everything from pork, to lamb to spareribs and this is served with the traditional mieliepap or maize meal porridge on the side. So that doesn't interest you, well, this culture has so much variation that you can find French, Indian, Portuguese, Dutch and Malay cuisine. Let your imagination be your guide but do think twice about Mashonzha. Why? It is cooked Mopani worms in a peri-peri sauce. We heard that, you said, "No Way." Our response, "yes worms!" You won't see your School of Flaunt founders trying that one!

And last but hardly least, pop down to New Zealand for a little Sauvignon Blanc. We didn't mention this hotel before but do try out the Lodge at Kauri Cliffs for hiking, pink beaches, some golf and sipping that Sauvignon Blanc at night! We can taste the fresh Kiwi's now, Yummy!

Unfortunately the only bad news with all of these trips is that you can not bring home cases of wine. You need an importer's license for that. A small note here: a friend from South Africa wanted to bring Mr. Smythe a few cases of wine as a little thank you for his hospitality in the states (Pre 9-11). Customs did not approve, no importer's license! The wine had to languish at one of the airlines until Mr. Smythe made some phone calls to appropriate friends at that airline. Strangely enough the wine was released to him with no duty necessary. Sometimes it's not what you know but whom you know. That goes for here as in other countries. Always keep those contacts that you make over the years. A little card here and there to let them know you are still thinking about them is a wise move. Alexandra and Cate always kept those cards they collected. A hotel room or dinner reservation is so much easier to attain when one has that little phone number of an influential person to call. Business and pleasure can co-mingle!

Our minds wander and daydream for there are so many countries to visit, so many bottles of wine to taste and so little time. We ask you, students, what is better than good food, great wine and beautiful scenery together? Bon Appetit!

**\*\*\*\***

Now let's just suggest that you are tired of flitting from one resort or country to the next and you really need to rest and relax. May we suggest cruising? Remember we are not talking cruising, as in a car, up and down Main Street, students! We are discussing ship-board fun. Yes, those huge wonderful sea going yachts, those kind that make your head turn! You may either purchase one or if you don't want the headaches of having another staff, captain, maintenance, and discussions about fuel costs to think about then charter with the best in the business. We like Meridian Yacht Charters www.meridianyachtcharters.com. Meridian will quickly and efficiently find the most luxurious yachts for your service anywhere in the world!

Example: Would you like something a little more intimate in the way of a yacht to charter? Then may we suggest the Lady Joy at 157 ft. She sleeps twelve guests, in seven bedrooms with a crew of nine. The Master suite includes a private office, walk in closets and his and her bathrooms. There are five additional staterooms and a nanny or children's cabin. PERFECT!! As for dining there is the Sun deck, Bridge deck or aft of the Main deck. You never have to have breakfast, lunch or dinner in the same spot! Wave runners, scooters, snorkel and scuba gear are yours for the using. And if you are worried about staying in shape there is also exercise equipment. All this for approximately $225,000 per week. We do wonder though, what would one do in a private office on vacation? Check email, perhaps? Oh how silly of us, one must always be able to check their stock portfolio!

If larger and more ocean going is your fancy, consider only the top cruise lines, such as Crystal, Seaborne or Regent Seven Seas. These ships could be considered a giant womb. Everything is done for you. Twenty-four hours a day a cheerful steward avails himself to your every whim! Please select a stateroom where you can spread out! If you have a certain champagne, special diet, or request, don't hesitate to notify the cruise line so all will be aboard before you arrive.

Remember, Bon Voyage parties can be ever so much fun, too! Have fresh flowers sent to your stateroom on a regular basis. This is a true SOF devotee wallowing in floating luxury. Do try the shipboard amenities from the spa, to pools, and skeet range. If you haven't tried skeet do! Old money loves it for venting frustrations. (Please refer to Lesson Eleven for Hobbies.) And last, but not least, remember cruising is a great way to shop. No need to worry about sending items from a foreign country, you just have them delivered to your floating home. Remember: Have staff or car and driver meet your ship and transport said purchases. Never schlep. Never ever SCHLEP!

**Note**: Be wary of the large "mall" ships. Even with the finest of accommodations, you will wait in lines, lines and more lines. You know we hate lines! Perhaps send the young ones on these ships with their Nanny or possibly suffer through it yourself as the doting parent or grandparent. We know they will have a good time. As for you, who needs ice skating, surfing and climbing walls? Climb Mount Everest if you want to climb a wall!

**Flaunt Flash News**: As we mentioned earlier cruising can be lovely. You can purchase your own yacht or go commercial but now South Korea's Samsung Heavy Industries along with Utopia Residences of Beverly Hills, California, is simply over the top with the world's most luxurious cruise ship. Total cost for this floating island is $1.1 billion. It measures over 971 feet long and is the largest passenger ship of this type to be built on the Asian continent.

You can actually own a home on this floating Shangrila. Owners? Yes, but only 200 residences will be available. As an owner, you may have a permanent home starting at 1,400 square feet for a mere $3.7 million dollars and if you need more room to stretch out you can have a 6,100 square foot home for $25 million. We aren't talking a week of time share here!

This unbelievable liner, named Utopia, how appropriate is that since Utopia means paradise, was built to tour the world. It will take its owners to some of the more lavish spots such as the Cannes Film Festival or on to Monte Carlo for the Grand Prix races and possibly some high-end gaming fun. Your forever "waterfront" home will tour ports in the world and your personal effects will always be on board. How simple life can be!

**Flaunt Flash News**: For those School of Flaunt devotees that might not be able to, nor even want to own a residence on the Utopia it will now offer a Luxury Hotel on board. Replete with retail boutiques, a casino, 500 seat theater, fine dining and more! Very important though, the "residence" areas will still be totally private. Look for a future date for launch! We will be there, will you?

As a small aside: since we are talking about traveling we must bring up luggage. Have you ever heard of a Henk suitcase? This "wheelie" and we hate to call it that was invented by a Dutchman, Henk van de Meene, who made a fortune in real estate in Europe. His suitcase was designed after he was forced to carry his own luggage at the height of a holiday period. Perish the thought but it does happen to the best of us. Not a Porter in site and the limo was late. Horrors! Presto the $20,000 suitcase was invented. Each case consists of 500 separate parts, fashioned from red Italian Burl, black ebony, horse hair, magnesium, aluminum, titanium, the finest leather and more. Doesn't sound like Samsonite to us!

Originally, Mr. Van de Meene was going to offer his limited edition for sale by invitation only. Now possibly Land Rover and Edmiston & Co., a specialist in the sale of charter and luxury yachts, may be trying to establish a cross marketing agreement for his $20,000 case on wheels? We understand that Mr. Van de Meene is currently working on a larger size model, a garment bag and even a golf bag. That would be total flaunt for our business tycoons, royalty and high profile celebrities! The Edmiston customer will be able to own a version of this case replete with the Edmiston logo. Check out: www. EdmistonCompany.com for more information.

For those of you who prefer Hermés, they have now come out with a fantastic new piece of luggage called the Orion. It is made of aluminum reinforced with carbon and Kevlar and the interior is lined in fine natural cowhide. Sounds divine and it is more reasonable at approximately $13,000. If need be this case also has a retractable handle and rollers for ease of use. Driver, bell captain, porter where are you?

Now we spoke earlier about the Edmiston Company. You simple must know this name, students. Nicholas Edmiston, an Englishman, is really the King of yacht brokers. No $3 million dollar yachts for him. He is dealing with selling 30 to 40 yachts per year with price tags as high as $135 million. From Saudi billionaires, movie stars, Russian new money business types and an occasional Royal, he sells them mega boats such as the 355 foot Lady Moura that has two retractable platforms, that come out of the side of the boat to make sand beaches. Heaven forbid that you would have to take a small boat to a beach to hang out! But just in case you don't want to be bothered with payrolls for staffing, Captains and maintenance expenses you can lease one of his boats called the Utopia (seems to be a catchy name) for $540,000 per week not including approximately $135,000, give or take a few thousand, for the food and service. Now remember a small point here, the Utopia is so big that you will have to rent a smaller vessel for getting back and forth to land and for anyone who you might like to invite for dinner. Merely a small inconvenience. So have the staff pack your tooth brush, swim suit and a few frocks. Fun is just a checkbook away.

****

Heaven forbid if you are prone to sea sickness, which you medically just cannot shake, or have seen the most recent Poseidon Adventure and it turned you off to cruising. If so we have some other fascinating vacation ideas.

Take a jet to Katmandu, Nepal, and ride an elephant up to Tiger Tops Resort. Please check to make sure that the current political atmosphere is safe before booking. Don't like Nepal but want to ride an elephant, go to Rajasthan, India, and stay at the Oberoi Vanyavilas and you can ride one there. Fly to Nairobi or Johannesburg and go on a 21 day safari with your own private guides and staff to set up your camp. Abercrombie and Kent is what we are thinking. Fabulous, absolutely smashing lodges and tented camps await you. Three of SOF's favorites are: the Earth Lodge at Sabi Sabi Private Game Reserve, Singita Sabi Sand Lodge at Kruger or just go to the Bushmans Kloof Wilderness Reserve and Wellness Retreat and relax. Bushmans is only three hours from Capetown.

No safari for you, no problem. Call the U.S. Ambassador to China and have him set up a tour for your family. Cruise the Amazon, the Nile, or balloon over France. Best of all, buy your own island or mega acreage and set up your own private resort replete with an 18 Hole Championship golf course. The Donald does this all the time! Trust us, students, we know of a wealthy individual who had a course built for himself in Illinois. Family, friends and business individuals were flown in for flaunt fun! Money sometimes is no object when you want to do something.

We never hesitate to give the SOF seal of approval to flying any-where in the world in your own private jet. Please remember to screen your potential flight attendants very carefully, though. We never want to see a Steven Slater type, popping the emergency slide and leaving with a bottle of your best champagne! That might have been enter-taining on You Tube but we don't want to see that happen to you!

Obviously having your own plane is always the simplest and easi-est way to travel but if you have to fly commercially, only First Class, please. We recommend: Singapore Airlines for service (try their Suites, beyond First Class), Lufthansa for on-time performance and American or United Airlines for domestic convenience. It goes with-out saying, immediately join the private clubs of the above airlines. At least when you are waiting for hours in between flights or during that delay for weather you can do it in the luxury of a decent chair with a beverage of your choice. Plus they have Wi-Fi for the harried business man who has to complete his next deal which could be you! Or per-haps you just want to upload some trip photos to your Facebook Page?

Lastly, there have been some innovative "shared or charter" jet companies that have been formed, but as an entrepreneur, you prob-ably knew that. Net Jets, Blue Star Jet, and Studio Jet are some of the best. But our favorite is the Greystone Aviation and Security Firm: http://www.greystoneaviationllc.com. Fasten your seat belts, stu-dents, this is going to be fun!!

**Flaunt Fiscal Travel Tip**: If you are currently unable to travel due to cost, think about a "Staycation" in your own home. Book some Spa Services, eat out for breakfast, lunch and dinner, sight see and do the museums in your own area! Your children will remember learning more about your home town.

# Lesson Seven Quiz

1. What amenities should your 4-5 Star Hotel offer?
    a. Limousine service
    b. Heated towel racks and bathroom floors
    c. Executive floor, replete with it's own cocktail lounge
    d. Twenty-four hour room service for your dog
    e. Private Butler
    f. All of the above

ANSWER: F

2. Where does the word POSH come from?
    a. Fancy Shmancy
    b. Port Ontario Senior Hospital
    c. A Secret Society at Yale
    d. Port Out, Starboard Home … for stateroom preference

ANSWER: D

3. When you arrive at your shipboard suite, first and foremost, you do what?
    a. Locate your life vest
    b. Accept the Captain's invitation to dine
    c. Order multiple floral arrangements for the cruise
    d. All of the above

ANSWER: D

4. What is the preferred minimum thread count for your hotel linens?
    a. 100
    b. 180
    c. 400
    d. 650

ANSWER: D – That will do nicely!

5. What is Tumi?
    a. The latest Sushi!
    b. Great Sea Sickness Rx
    c. Top flight luggage for the discerning traveler
    d. The Vietnamese version of the name "Tommy"

ANSWER: C – If it is not totally speaking School of Flaunt to you and then there is always Hermés or Henk.

6. When is it time to upgrade your luggage?
    a. When you see a scuff mark
    b. When you tire of the color
    c. When your staff starts carrying the same luggage
    d. All of the above

ANSWER: D – Especially if A should happen!

7. Quick! Which key resorts did we speak of in Lesson Seven? Which hotels did we recommend in San Francisco. If you are unable to name at least four then reread this Lesson. You are not ready to go anywhere!

# LESSON EIGHT:
## Transportation and Motoring Vehicles
"Worth School of Flaunt Mention"

TRANSPORTATION SHOULD ABOVE all, be a pleasure. Indulge yourself in any number of ways with a Mercedes, Bentley, Porsche or Rolls Royce, top of the line models preferably for getting around town. If you are into the fast imports, such as Ferrari or Lamborghini, they will definitely put you out in front of the crowd. Certain old-money, banking people have been known to get a Lamborghini for every one in their immediate family. We so hate jealous, petty family fights over something as trivial as the family car! The aforementioned surely takes care of that tedious problem!

Now remember accessories are always a must. These are some of the must haves and in fact as far as we are concerned givens for your favorite little get around car: high-end stereo speakers, fine leather seats, GPS Mapping component, Sirius radio, heated and cooled seats, tinted windows, "Bluetooth," Autonet Mobile and the ability to be able to hear Tweets while driving. If money is no object you may want to just upgrade to a Maybach 62 Zepplin which comes replete with a built in atomizer that diffuses your favorite fragrance throughout the cabin. Luxury does have a price tag though and this little cutie will run you around $500,000. For approximately $1.8 mil you can upgrade to a Cinque Roadster but if that still doesn't impress you then there is the

Bugatti Veyron 16.4 Grand Sport or the Koenigsegg CCXR which are both around $2,000,000. True SOF flaunt.

Continuing on, students, it has been said that your car can say a lot about you. Some cars say, "I've got it" while others infer that you are not the flashy type but are well educated. San Diego-based market research company, Strategic Vision, released data in 2009 that 70% of Honda owners have a college degree or higher.

**Flaunt Flash News**: Eco-friendly, high gas mileage vehicles are driven by celebs as well as millionaires, too, so you might want to re-think your wheels. Or you can be really eccentric and drive older models like some of our billionaires do. Allegedly billionaire Warren Buffett is driving his 2006 Cadillac DTS, Ikea founder Ingvar Kamprad still has his '93 Volvo 240 GL and Jim Walton, owner of Wal-Mart gets around town in a 2002 Dodge Dakota. Enough said!

****

So does all of that sound rather the same, Mercedes to Porsche, rather Ho-Hum nothing different or special? Well, it is time to attend a Barrett-Jackson Collector Car auction. Yes, you are off to Scottsdale, Palm Beach, Las Vegas or Orange County in California for one of their renowned events. Pack your bags and the check books because their docket has some of the most diverse "little buggies" in the world to bid on. From vehicles like John Dillinger's getaway car, a 1930 Ford Model A Coupe, to Shelby Cobras and a broader range of motoring vehicles for everyone's pocket book, you will find there is something for all.

Even if you don't want to purchase a car, watching the bidding is fascinating. In 2007, a 1966 Shelby Cobra 427 "Super Snake" sold for $5,000,000, in 2006, a 1953 Chevrolet Corvette "#003" convertible went for a mere $1,080,000 and in 2008, a 1970 Ford Mustang Boss 429 fastback went for $205,700. Now you regret not hanging onto that first car, or Mommy and Daddy selling what was to become a collector's item! Well so be it, nothing you can do about it now. Here is a tissue, wipe off those tears. Get yourself under control!

**Flaunt Fiscal Tip**: We want you to think about this, students. The above vehicles all come with some type of story or history and remember we told you that people love a "good" story. So you can't afford one of these dream vehicles or even the new Rolls Royce but you need something with a story. Buy that older model Rolls or Bentley. Here's the story: you have a very eccentric great Uncle who just died and left you his Rolls. You just don't have the heart to sell it because it belonged to him. So you can now be the eccentric and drive that old beauty. You'll still make heads turn because you are in a Rolls. We don't recommend doing this with an old VW Beetle! Use some judgment here, students. Now go out and find an oldie but goodie!

**Flaunt Fiscal True Story**: A very good friend purchased a 944 Porsche, year 1986 for $300. Yes only $300, but he did have to put $35,000 in restomodded costs into it. But does it look great now! And such a story, "I bought this car for $300." He'll have that car forever. A new Porsche is how much?

As we have mentioned so many times it is important to understand the lingo of whatever you are attending. From Wikipedia: Restoration is sometimes confused with the term "restomod." A restomod replaces some portions of the car as they were when the car was first offered for sale and changes (updates) others. If any part of the car is not as it was offered for sale, the car has been "restomodded" and not restored. A restoration puts a car in the same condition as when it was first offered for sale. Always do you home work!

O.K., so still in doubt about your automobile, this is easy to remedy. The limousine is what you are after. You owe it to yourself to wallow in success and hire a full time chauffeur. The cost of such motoring grandeur will be negligible because every day will become a holiday from driving. It also provides a buffer zone between you and life's little nasty encounters, such as rude cab and bus drivers, trying to find change for the toll booth and stopping for gas. Nothing can be more time consuming or tiring for busy entrepreneurs than having to spend valuable time doing the driving yourself! Remember one of the perks of having risen to the level of CEO at a Fortune 500 company is that limo and driver. Something to strive for, students.

**Flaunt Flash News**: You may now get a Ferrari Limo. We are not fooling with you! Yes they take a Ferrari and cut it in half. The front of your limo looks like the front of a Ferrari as well as the back. And guess what? It still goes down the road at over 150 MPH! Yikes now that is "FAST, FLAUNT, FUN!" Customization does have it costs though, think $400,000 but remember your driver does deserve some fun, too.

Remember these are "must" options for your limo: telephone, intercom system, television, bar replete with crystal glassware and refrigerator, writing desk in burl wood with enough room for your laptop, heated and cooled seats with back massage, and your own open glass roof. All these items and why you need them should be self explanatory! Just in case there would ever be a mechanical problem in cold weather do keep a fox throw handy or at the very least a cashmere blanket. Last and be it not least, don't forget a small china box filled with dog cookies for your favorite canine companion. The only time we want to see you pulling through a fast food establishment in your limo is when your 4-legged baby might need a hamburger fix. O.K., you can have one, too. We do so love In and Out Burger!

We would not think this necessary but under no circumstances should you have mud flaps, fringe of any sort, boom-box speakers, neon lights, small bobble heads, dice or bumper stickers on any vehicle you own. NEVER!

Personalized plates are totally acceptable. Example: Smythe 1 or the name of your business or estate.

****

Continuing with transportation this takes us to air travel. If you do a lot of traveling, you should really own your own jet. Preferably something that sleeps at least four has a bathroom with a shower, a conference area, good galley and all the latest safety systems for the cockpit. Naturally you must have your own pilots as in plural and one flight attendant, so that you can be free to socialize or conduct important business. Oh, it is just like "Up, Up and Away In Your Beautiful Balloon." Perfection.

Bottom line on this topic: a private jet is convenient, keeps you out of the fray in airport security lines, having to submit to countless delays, airport screeners rummaging through your luggage and possible body pat downs (perish the thought). You fly when and where you want at all times and your pilots handle your luggage from your car to the plane. No they really do, students. Would this happen on a commercial airliner? Ha, you can't even get a decent meal let alone someone to help you with your luggage.

No more enduring the idiot behind you who keeps kicking the back of your seat, the other bozo who has his head set on as loud as it can go so that you can enjoy their choice of music, NOT, and last of all the screaming babies! All should be a distant, ugly memory!

**Flaunt Fiscal Tip**: Remember, students, you can also lease out your plane and crew helping to defray the costs and using it as a business write-off. O.K., so you cannot afford your own "gazillion" dollar jet? … Consider Net Jets or Blue Star Jets for personal private jetting. Packages and part time ownership are available and actually can be practical. If you are only interested in chartering, Greystone Aviation is a wonderful way to go.

Ghastly thought but sometimes it does happen, you must travel commercial, please do so in first class. We know that it is not what it was in its heyday of coast to coast flying with 6 course dinners, replete with appetizers, soup, salad cart, carved Chateaubriand at your seat, followed by a cheese course, and then lastly dessert, but at least you might have some extra leg room and hopefully no screaming baby nearby. Pray that another business man is seated next to you and all he would like to do is work on his computer! Pull out your eye shades, neck pillow and place those noise abating head sets over your ears and go to sleep! Your misery hopefully will be over in a few hours.

****

We feel that it is again necessary to comment on motor homes. We are not talking about dragging an RV behind your Dodge Ram, students. Think Marathon Coach! For a mere $2,000,000 you can ride in style. What do you get for this price? Well, this is a luxury bus conversion with everything including the kitchen sink! 42'' Plasma TV in the salon and 32'' LCD in the bedroom, leather furniture, marble in the bathroom, wood plank floors, ceiling fans, wall sconces, temperature sensing shower valves, intercom and camera at the front door and even a Sub-Zero refrigerator. The list of upgrades goes on and on. They do have models in stock so you can drive off immediately if you like.

They are big and grand and sleep a veritable crowd, but please, students, unless you are a country western singer or Whoopi Goldberg, only use these vehicles for taking crowds of friends to major sporting events. Make sure you have an experienced designated driver and then let the fun begin as you do a little tail-gate celebrating at your Alma Mater. God forbid, do not take an actual vacation in one. Good grief we can hear you screaming now, "But I want to drive across country and see all of the National Parks." O.K., go! But be prepared to draw a crowd when you park that buggy at the Grand Canyon. And just remember we told you so!

****

If you are into boating you should consider having a sail boat made in Hong Kong! Trust us many do and oddly their boats never seem to be registered in the U.S.A. We will make no further comment about that tactic. Just make sure you have plenty of teak throughout and monogrammed items for your galley and bathrooms.

There are also Swan sailboats, which are worthy SOF craft, too, but do realize that sailing can become addictive. Some have even described sailors as, Sailing Nuts. But looking into our SOF crystal ball we see the Rolex Cup in your future. Now that is true SOF fun!

Not into sailing and want more creature comforts? Big and comfy, simply buy the mega-yacht. Do remember they usually take three to five years to even take your order for a new custom design, but resales are available that have been totally refitted. One would never know they had been previously owned. And remember we are all about getting a deal, students. If you can work one do it! Wonder what happened to Bernie Madoff's?

Lastly on this topic, usual rule of thumb to use is, are you looking for under 130' or over 130'? Price point for under 130' is probably between $3,000,000 to $12,000,000 whereas over 130' will be $20,000,000 and up!

School of Flaunt students, we are having an out of body experience. Did we die and go to SOF Heaven or Hell? Are aliens ready to come out of Russian billionaire, Andrey Meinichenko's $300,000,000 yacht? Designed by Philippe Starck this mega-yacht makes some swoon and others shriek. This is the definition of unique from it's name which is simply A to it's submarine like figure. The A has six guest suites with movable, leather-covered walls to create larger suites if necessary and the master bedroom is located on A's super tower. Andrey and his wife have a bed on a turntable for panoramic views and rumor has it that they have a separate and private area for those romantic moments. Wonder if they put out a Do Not Disturb sign on the door? Something tells me they probably have another system to tell the staff not to bother them.

But we digress, need some entertainment on the A? How will three swimming pools and three 30' speedboats do? You will need these since most of A's design eliminates decks for lounging. Well, everyone to their own. Because of A's totally different approach to a mega-yacht that is why some really think it is totally SOF and others think it is not. Bet Andrey doesn't care what the rest of the world thinks about his yacht! That is the purest form of SOF. Where is the bubbly? Let's have a toast to him.

Now if $300,000,000 is simply over the top for you then think more reasonable. Something like the Linda Lou for $100,000,000. This mega-yacht has five decks and 8,500 sq. ft. of luxury cabin space to wallow in. But be forewarned, students, plan to spend 10% of the cost of your yacht every year for maintenance, staff and of course your monogrammed soaps for your water home. Don't say that we didn't tell you. You know we hate whining.

Continuing merrily along let us discuss "choppers" otherwise known as motorcycles. Frankly SOF does not endorse them because they can be so dangerous but lets face it, students, there is nothing like exploring the back roads of the country on those SOF beasts of speed. Wind in your face, that feeling of freedom, custom leather jacket, helmet and leather gloves. Just a touch of that bad boy side of you to flaunt. We must admit you are slightly sexy but then we digress. So, if you really have to have one, it should be done as a custom order. Expect to pay anywhere from $100,000 plus and maybe even up to a million for those wheels. Not kidding here, students. Think middle eastern money where money is no object.

Where to shop? Try Orange County Choppers who build bikes around themes for corporate or celebrity customers. Even the United States Air Force has commissioned a bike to the tune of $150,000 with them. We know tax payer money but they use it for community outreach programs. Otherwise probably known as recruiting but let's get back to this bike. It is 10' long and is modeled after the F-22 Raptor complete with the Air Force symbol rims, riveted gas tank, Raptor exhausts and rear view mirrors in the shape of jets. Wow, now we are talking a real bike for collectors. They also have a limited edition production line where prices start at only $31,000. Such a deal! Especially when you compare it to a MV Agusta F4 CC, Italian built, which runs around $140,000. Its top speed is 195 MPH and each bike has it own platinum plate located near the steering column showing the model number from 1 to 100. Va-va-vroom!

Just please have lots of driving lessons before you take that muscle vehicle out on the road. Lauren Hutton (famous model) can tell you about spending some time in the hospital because of her Harley accident! We don't want that for any of you.

**** 

**Flaunt Fiscal Tip**: We realize that many of you might not be able to afford luxury vehicles or yachts. Please, dear students, have a safe car, a clean car and use your seatbelts.

And our last SOF transportation thoughts, on something that is sooooo, well at the very least repugnant, are dirt bikes. Please have someone shoot you on sight if you ever think of purchasing one!

# Lesson Eight Quiz

1. On what occasions should you use a limousine?
    a. Weddings
    b. Funerals
    c. Grocery Shopping
    d. All of the above

ANSWER: D


2. Which of the following modes of transport are unacceptable?
    a. Lamborghini
    b. Falcon 4000
    c. Bentley
    d. None of the above

ANSWER: D – Trick question to make sure you are really reading the question.


3. Which of the following modes of transport are acceptable?
    a. Dirt Bike
    b. Greyhound Bus
    c. Hitch hiking
    d. Absolutely none of the above

ANSWER: D – If you answered correctly you are now reading the questions.


4. What basics should complete your limousine?
    a. Baccarat Crystal and Dom Perignon
    b. Reading Lights

    c. Corn Chips, Onion Dip and Boxed Wine
    d. A & B
    e. A & C

ANSWER: D – If you answered C, we are talking serious indigestion!

5. When flying commercial, what is the first thing you should do?
    a. Have your assistant buy your First Class ticket and contact the station manager so they can be there to assist you.
    b. Scream for a skycap and drop your Louis Vuitton luggage at the curb!
    c. Have the Captain and his crew members personally assist you with your luggage.
    d. Any of the above
    e. A & B
    f. A & C

ANSWER: A

6. Which two yachts did we mention in Lesson Nine?
    a. The Bang and The Olufsen
    b. The Dolce and The Gabbana
    c. The Linda Lou and The A
    d. The Laverne and The Shirley

ANSWER: C – If you answered this incorrectly go back and read this lesson three times! There is only so much we can contend with!

## LESSON NINE:
## Politics, Charities, Clubs
"The Human Side of SOF"

WITHOUT GETTING MAUDLIN, some people do need our help. Disease and poverty are still running rampant throughout the world and it is our SOF policy to always help wherever we can. It is our debt to society to assist the less fortunate. With the downturn in our economy and the burst of the "Living Large Bubble," we all know someone who has suffered. You may find this hard to believe, but there are families of four that have to exist on less than $10,000 per year. So, if you are among the many who have the ability to give back now is the time to step forward. Not only will you be helping mankind but in your altruistic endeavors you will add meaning to your life, as well.

You might not be aware but old money very quietly underwrites many of their hometown institutions to the tune of hundreds of millions of dollars. If you are truly new money, read on.

The epitome of "elegant" and "unpretentious" but always with that air of a "regal" grand dame of society would describe Ms. Louise Dieterle Nippert, who along with her husband Louis "Gus" Nippert, who was a great grandson of James Gamble, founder of Procter & Gamble Co., have contributed anonymous gifts estimated in the hundreds of millions of dollars. In late 2009, Mrs. Nippert gave back once again to her beloved home town of Cincinnati. $85 million dollars was announced as a gift to the Louise Dieterle Nippert Musical Arts Fund to help support the Cincinnati Symphony Orchestra, Opera and Ballet Company and other arts organizations. This was a public display of support but for years the Nippert family had quietly supported the arts financially behind the scenes as well as other charitable endeavors.

Her husband's family contributed the money to build Nippert Stadium at the University of Cincinnati in 1923 after the death of a family member in a football injury. Some family members belonged to the Sigma Alpha Epsilon fraternity at the university as well. Why do we bring this up? Because we want you to understand how old money lives. This will open the doors of opportunity for you. Take our well-heeded advice here. Remember, education, clubs, charities, movers and shakers in your community are all entwined. Please read on, students.

We suggest that you start today with the charity of your choice but get thyself on a board or preferably two ASAP because they are wonderful ways of helping mankind. These boards are a great deal of fun and wield soooo much power, too! Believe us, heads do snap to attention when you say that you are on certain boards. Key boards are usually the following: Museums, Symphonies, Ballet Companies and Major Hospitals. Remember medical research is so very important and if you are known to be on said hospital board this can be your foray into helping you garner quick appointments with top docs if you or a family member becomes ill. The old adage always holds true: it is not what you know but whom you know. Just ask Peachy Deegan! Ms. Deegan is the new "Hedda Hopper" of NYC. Sample her signature cocktail at Swifties on the Upper East Side! Flauntilicious!

Usually you must be invited to join said boards. How to do this? Just attend an event, write a large check, purchase a table, etc., … and you will be noticed. At that point invitations will be forthwith, we promise.

The second way, believe it or not, is to be a vocal supporter of that organization. Support them through your other endeavors. Yes, you are reading right! You are involved with another group but you use your influence with the first group to help support the board you would like to be invited to join. They want people on boards who are very visible in the community. One more reason to make sure that your picture is in the newspaper. Note here: many a Publicity Chair has fallen into the heady trap of putting her own picture in Town and Country or the local society page once too often. Beware, students, of appearing "too grasping for notice" … it does not bode well.

Back to basics, do your part and pat yourself on the back! Yes, we know self-serving, but bottom line is you will be helping others as well as yourself. Looks like a win-win for all! Just a little aside here, we said purchase a table at an event. Why? Your name is in the catalogue for the large donation. Voila! You are now top drawer!

Once you have joined the board of choice, do offer to Chair the biggest and best events. Then promptly delegate, delegate, delegate. Avoid Co-Chairing as too much consulting is involved. We speak from experience here, students. As the single Chair, your word should be the rule in deciding on details of the event. Your fellow board members will help with execution and you reap the adulation. Brilliant! Don't decorate the ballroom, organize it! Don't run the auction, plan it! Always the innovator because you are the true SOF'er; organized, sophisticated and successful in everything you seek to undertake!

Remember if your 501c3 has a Director and staff that is salaried, do make them earn their money, but treat them with the highest respect. They are there to make your life easier by working behind the scenes to help make the event a success.

****

Let us tell you about a true SOF event that would be hard to copy but "wow" does this one make a statement. It is called the Pebble Beach Concours d'Elegance. This is where cars, charity and the truly rich and famous meet. It could probably be considered the most prestigious event of its kind. What is it you ask? It is the "finale" of a week long festival of classic car events in the Monterey, California, area.

Concours d'Elegance, which is French for a "competition of elegance," is an event for both pre-war and post-war collector cars that are judged for their authenticity. Cars come from all over the world to compete and many collectors have spent years and hundreds of thousands of dollars purchasing and restoring a car in hopes of winning. The competing cars can be valued up into the millions.

Deemed to be a gathering for the very wealthy and their guests, plus thousands of attendees, this extravaganza has raised millions for the United Way of Monterey County, the Pebble Beach Company Foundation and other local and national organizations. Are you getting the "concept" here, students?

Foundations can be fun to work on, they can be your entry for meeting interesting people while doing something for the less fortunate, and possibly opening doors of society to you. We would like to add here that this would make a fabulous little vacation jaunt. Cars, some golf and drive that 17 mile scenic drive. Pack your bags now!

****

But getting back to chairing an event. Do invite all your friends to the Gala affair and encourage them, if necessary, into making donations. You may or may not care to solicit donations from shops and services. We, at SOF, feel that this should be delegated as well, but you can help your committee people if you simply take the time to hand write a personal note to all those establishments. When they realize you have taken the time to write them personally, they will fully realize the importance of your project!

Finally, enjoy yourself! Float around the event meeting and greeting with the poise and polish that we hope you have learned in previous lessons. Have your publicity photos taken and spend oodles of money! And, again we repeat, always remember you are helping your fellow mankind and don't forget it is a write-off too. (See your Tax Attorney.)

Another piece of Flaunt advice: after the successful event do have the board and all of your committee heads to your home for a recognition cocktail party. And under no circumstances should you forget that all volunteers be sent a lovely note of appreciation. Kudos should not be spared!!

We would like to add one more story about Charity events. Most of the time you will find that they will have live auctions and silent auctions for wonderful donated items such as vacations, tickets to major sporting events or private dinners with a celebrity to mention only a few. One old-money family who owned a sky box for years at a major stadium donated their box for one of the games, along with a catered dinner for 20 to be auctioned off. Big money was offered for this and the happy winners looked forward to inviting 20 of their friends for the game. The donors hired a caterer for the party and thought that the affair was now organized. What to their chagrin happened? The caterer cancelled the day of the game. We do not kid you here. Obviously this caterer would not be catering any longer in that town unless it was for a local circus passing through! But getting back to the story, when the couple heard that the caterer had cancelled they raided their estate garden, cooked food for 20 people and took it immediately to their stadium sky box . They dressed down and when asked who they were they simply said, "Oh the cook and server. We hope that you enjoy your meal and the game." No one ever knew that they were being waited on by some of the oldest money in town. Remember, students, you can't let your charities down!

Hard work, generosity, and understatement are all hallmarks of the super wealthy in most cases. Of course this needs to be instilled in your children from generations past and present. No slackers in the SOF family tree! (Please consult Lesson Six for SOF Manners and Attitude.)

**Flaunt Fiscal Tip**: If one cannot afford to write a Big Check for your charity, fear not. Volunteer to help at the Charity office or function setup. No excuses and you will feel so much better helping others. Remember those that "Show Up" for "Set Up" are noted. And those who "do not or think this is below their station" are showing bad form again. Tacky!

****

Proceeding along we must step into the area of politics. They go hand in hand with power, social acceptability and SOF. Many a political contribution has brought social acceptability. Vote for whomever you will, but always be in the party that is currently in OFFICE. We know one lady who dined regularly with the Bush family and promptly became the biggest Democrat in DC when the Clintons came to town. This flipping can be tricky, but it goes with the territory of being a Grand Dame in DC. Small aside: beware of any politician that is fixated on HAIR, as in the unfortunate former Illinois Governor. No elaboration needed.

Now from the time you are old enough to walk and talk, everyone should work to get into the BEST clubs. Remember life is a series of special groups, from the exclusive country clubs to Phi Beta Kappa. Your club says a lot about you. When your children are in college, they should pledge the best sororities and fraternities. In Texas, these connections are made at summer camps. It is said that "Camp Waldemar Girls" can select any Texas sorority they choose! This starts at age eight, students. Also encourage the kids to strive for honoraries, such as Mortar Board or Phi Beta Kappa. Think of those Secret Societies at the Ivies. Interesting, you bet! Some of our Presidents and top politicians have made these clubs high priority.

Influence those Junior SOF'ers to join the young Democrats, Republicans or other party of their choice. The most important thing is that they learn to vote! Mom may join the Democratic or Republican Women's Club and the League of Women Voters. If you find that it is just too socially stressful to be politically active, then you can register as an Independent. We all know they are gaining in acceptance and you will probably be courted by both political parties. You can write checks to all and keep everyone happy. That might be the way to go! You can be Switzerland in a political world of acrimony.

Never forget there is always the Junior League or "The League" as it is known in the South, and the enriching work with the local symphony, art museum, or children's charities where you can also be involved. Besides obviously making you a better, well-rounded person, we cannot accentuate the importance of these endeavors for meeting and greeting the movers and shakers in your communities, e.g., the Rockefeller's, Vanderbilt's and the Getty's of "your home town." All could be important to getting little Alex or Alexandra into their school of choice later in their lives. (Please consult Lesson Ten on schooling.)

Lastly, display those diplomas, plaques and awards proudly. Hang those fraternity ties around your neck! And give back! Here is a true story of how hanging your Sorority membership in a framed picture helped take one from just being another guest to being the hostess's new best friend.

The hostess was a Grand Dame of old money in the South. Alexandra was trying to find the powder room in the rather large expanse of the home when she happened to notice a framed award from "her" sorority acknowledging that said Grand Dame had been a member for fifty years. Oh, what a nugget she had just discovered. When she returned to the party she walked over to the Grand Dame and said, "Miss Ilean may I have your hand?" Miss Ilean looked slightly confused but extended her hand and Alexandra slipped her the secret grip. Our Grand Dame looked at her and then asked, "Well, darling, are you a member of my sorority?" And Alexandra nodded yes. From that minute on Alexandra was just not a guest but her new best friend. Miss Ilean was in her glory now, introducing Alexandra as her sorority sister to one and all. Heed our words well, as we said earlier: all is intertwined, money, social status, schools, and clubs.

We must add here a major FLAUNT FAILURE! Never lie about being in any organization, fraternity, sorority or honorary. It will eventually catch up with you. Remember it is a small world. Recently a new acquaintance said that he was in a certain fraternity at a certain college. When this information was passed on in a friendly conversation to a third party who went to the same Alma Mater they immediately said, "Well then he certainly would have known Ted." The third party checks out the person in the Alumni catalogue and then looks up class pictures in the school's yearbook. Sorry, no mention of this person as a member of said fraternity. His name was removed from future invitees. If he had only been honest and said he had graduated from said college, but no, he had to embellish his resume. No saving face there, students.

## Lesson Nine Quiz

1. Which of the following is not a national fraternity or sorority?
    a.  Delta Delta Delta
    b.  Sigma Alpha Epsilon
    c.  Alpha Sigma Sigma

ANSWER: C – ASS, puh-leese! Learn the Greek alphabet.


2. What is the Junior League famous for?
    a.  A Cook Book
    b.  Philanthropy Work
    c.  Luncheons and Fashion Shows (all replete with boneless baked chicken)
    d.  All of the Above

ANSWER: D


3. What is the name of your local Democratic and Republican committee person? Phone Number?

    If you cannot give us these names and numbers, the simplest of our requests, you must get them immediately and then contribute generously to their local candidates.


4. In Lesson Ten, which was NOT a suggested way of joining an "Elite Charity Women's Board"?
    a.  A GENEROUS DONATION
    b.  Purchase a Table for an Event
    c.  See and Be Seen
    d.  Blackmail

ANSWER: D – We never break the law. End of story.

5. What did we warn you about if you happen to be the Publicity Chair?
    a. Wear something photogenic and slimming
    b. Carry a clipboard for jotting down names of spouses
    c. Drag the Society Photographer around by his tie
    d. Do not put your own "ONLY" photo in all the publications, bad form, that one

ANSWER: D

# LESSON TEN:
## Montessori to Med School

"Only the Strong Survive!"

ANY SOF PARENT should be aware of the importance of a proper education and no scrimping in this area! We recommend being progressive, but sticking to those private institutions if your pocket book can afford it. Don't short change your little darlings and think how adorable they'll look in their uniforms! And it is a wonderful way to start a family tradition. Grandfather or Grandmother attended, you attended, how could they not admit little Jimmy or Jennifer?

We know that Europe offers a number of fine boarding schools and this obviously gives you another reason to shop abroad, but many fine institutions are right here in the North East. Have you ever heard of the TSAO (Ten Schools Admission Organization)? It is a group of leading American secondary schools and was established in 1956. It includes the following schools, Choate RoseMary Hall, Phillips Academy (known as Andover), Phillips Exeter Academy (known as Exeter), Deerfield Academy, St Paul's School, Hotchkiss School, Lawrenceville School, Taft School, Loomis Chaffee and The Hill School. Any of these will help get you into a Harvard, Princeton, Yale or Cornell to mention only a few. Fees for these schools run approximately $45,000 per year for boarders and $35,000 for day students. Most are co-educational. Please remember these names and if you hear them mentioned it is another opportune time to nod in approval.

If you think these schools are all about money and not education you are wrong! The curriculum usually ranges from economics, mathematics, philosophy, religion to mention only a few, with internships in academic research to visual and performing arts. You never can tell when your little darling might be invited to perform at the White House or Westminster Abbey since most have orchestras and choral groups. Your children could be mingling with future presidents of the United States, e.g., as John F. Kennedy and Kings in the Middle East, to actresses such as Jamie Lee Curtis or designers like Vera Wang. Recently we saw the King of Jordan being interviewed at Deerfield Academy, upon doing some research we found that the King went there when he was a young man. Could it be that his children now attend?

If you don't want your little one to go off to boarding school then do research in your area about top schools. For example in New York (Manhattan) there is the Chapin School. Now this is for our daughters where they can begin in kindergarten and go through the 12th grade. Tuition runs around $35,000 per year but Chapin is ranked approximately 14th at sending students to Harvard University. And sometimes it's not what you know but whom you know or having that one little extra piece of paper from a Prep school to help you along. Harsh but true.

Please do your homework carefully since you are not only spending the big bucks but you want them to pay off in the long run for your children. If it requires donating to get them in, then donate, donate, donate! Help them build a new building or at the very least, a new soccer field and make sure it carries your family name.

**Flaunt Fiscal Tip**: Now don't despair if you can't afford the tuition or donations. These schools also have need-based financial aid and merit scholarships or tuition loans with financing programs. Where there is a will, there will always be a way!

The new friends your little ones will make acquaintance with will astound you! Extend a holiday home to those abandoned youngsters at your school. Alas, sadly even in the best families it happens. You may find out that he or she might be a young sheik or daughter of a CEO you've been dying to meet! Or your child might be invited to their home or summer place for vacation, too. Reciprocation remember that, you never can tell who you will meet. You might even consider a few years in school overseas for them. Lugano and San Moritz aren't bad places for you to visit your children. Plus it will help polish a second language for them which is a total must!

True story: A good friend had her son enrolled in Exeter. He went to visit a friend (another Exeter student) on Long Island. When she went to pick him up, the hostess invited her to stay for their barbecue. Who happened to be coming later in the afternoon since her daughter (Chelsea) was also at the party? Hillary Clinton. Yes, Senator Clinton was not Senator at the time but was running for the office in the state of New York. One thing leads to next and Hillary tells her that she and Bill were going to be in another part of New York campaigning. Our friend mentioned that her family lived there and that was where she is going after the party. Well, Hillary invites her, her husband and son to join Chelsea, Bill and herself the next night for dinner after she had finished her campaign stops. There they were having dinner with the former President, soon to be Senator and now Secretary of State. All because some children attended the same school.

Now just think of Kate Middleton, the Duchess of Cambridge and future Queen of England. Think that union would have happened if her parents had not enrolled her in private schools and a top ranked University? Remember we aren't talking a junior college here, students! Reality check!!

We seriously doubt that Prince William looked for a wife in the local pub! O.K., he might have picked her up in a local college pub but would he have considered her marriage material with a lack of credentials? There are commoners and then there are commoners! Kate came with credentials!

Lastly, it is a small world, students. Remember you have to watch everything you say and do. Think we are kidding here, NOT! It is scary how you will run into people around the world. Cell phone cameras be damned! Whether in a restaurant or on an elevator. Always be prepared!

We told you before that all is intertwined: e.g., education, clubs, zip codes and politics. So do get those children into the right schools for yourself and their futures, too! You could be dining with former Presidents, Senators or Secretaries of State. That's not too shabby. (Please refer to Lesson Six on manners.)

**\*\*\*\***

So you are now pondering the question of college, a master's program or possible medical school for your little one. Yikes a small fortune for all. How could you afford one of these elite private prep schools with all the costs of college? Possibly they are out of the question. Can we take you back to Lesson Four, students? Remember Zip Code, Location, Address?

What do these have to do with our topic of schools? Unfortunately the better public learning institutions, i.e., high schools, are usually located in those more affluent areas. As we said before, you are better off to live in the smallest house in the community with the best Zip code. Why is life always about Location, Location, Location? A question to ponder but we do not have time for a philosophical discussion. Just remember our words of wisdom and purchase in the right neighborhood.

Now it is also very important if you are going the way of public education that you encourage your child to excel. They should of course join clubs that will look good on the admission form and lots of community service. We know that they all can't play a sport and be good at it, but if at all possible get them on the golf team. Golf scholarships are great and sometimes the entrance to Stanford. So get those lessons and golf clubs now for little junior. Your child could end up playing with the future Tiger Woods. Remember he attended Stanford. We know Tiger has had his own problems to deal with but there will be the next "Tiger" and your child could be him or her or at the very least continue a friendship over the years with that illustrious pro. You could be traveling on that pro's yacht, we can think of worse things to do.

We would also like to add that your daughters should know how to play golf. Why? Please don't be naive here. Where do you think those business deals are put together? On the course or afterwards over dinner! Not on some TV show! Forgive us, Shark Tank.

Your daughters must also be prepared not to be left out of the Boys' Club called the golf course. Plus it is fun to beat them or "let" them win by one stroke. You, ladies, can beat them up over the deal later because they think they can beat you. One upmanship, ladies, it can be so much fun! As The Donald said, "It is the art of the deal." And parents do remember you must join that golf club and learn to play well, too. You can always meet someone who might help you get your child into their Alma Mater. Just a thought, students. We have to work all of the angles here.

Now if your child is not a scholar don't despair. TUTORS! Worth every cent. Find that "area" that your child loves and encourage them. This also is a way into the best schools. We do remember a friend who was a mediocre student but excelled as an artist. That high school portfolio got her into Carnegie Mellon. Not too shabby. Where there is a will there is a way!

If your child has decided that a larger, public University is where they absolutely have to go it might be easier on your pocket book but they really should join a fraternity or sorority. Movers and shakers on campus are generally members of these organizations. It is amazing when you have on your glass ring with your fraternity Greek letters engraved in the stone how many will notice. Then if they, too, were a member, they slip you the secret grip and you are automatically their new best friend. At the very least it does give you some common ground and it is a great way to start a conversation. Example: a President of J.C Penny was a Delta Tau Delta member at a public institution (not a junior college) and was always a mover and shaker on campus. We're sure this didn't hurt him in his climb up the corporate ladder. He and his wife, a Delta Delta Delta sorority member, just gave $10,000,000 to the university they graduated from. Again, students, another example about how all is intertwined! Education, clubs, zip code, etc.

We must also give you a little advice. So many times we have seen many parents give in to the child about where they want to go to school or what their major should be. Unless that child has been born into old money, which we spoke about previously, their major is very important. Yes, you are going to send them to that prestigious school and you hear them tell you that they want to get a degree in Anthropology. It is a simple answer for those of you who haven't established a trust fund for them to live off of for the rest of their lives, "not on my dime!" Trust us we have seen many of our friends spend the big bucks for their children's education, for the child never to use it.

Children have wonderful ideas about how they want to save the world. We are not suggesting that you squelch their dreams but you have to be realistic. He or she can save the world after they have made their way in the world. Please be very careful when letting your child choose their college or major. If they throw down the gauntlet and say, "I won't go to college if I can't have my way." Well, again like you treat a three year old, call their bluff! Get a spine and tell them they can go out and get a job, start paying you rent, pay for their cellphone, car insurance and clothes. Option number two, they can go to a great college and get an education in something that will lead to a "real" job!

Lastly parents, NO excuses! It is your job to try to get those kids into top learning institutions. Remember, you don't have to take NO for an answer. If their grades are unacceptable get them a tutor; then make those phone calls to friends that might help, and as we said before you can always donate, build a Library or start an endowment. How can they turn Junior away? Example: We have noted that Notre Dame is famous for admitting per building. Check out all the SOF family names on the buildings when you visit the campus. True!

We wish you the best of luck if need be! Start planning now!

**Flaunt Fiscal Tip**: Save early for your young one's education. Fill out a FAFSA form online, and speak with a good Financial Planner to help with Student Loans, Grants and Scholarships. It works!

## Lesson Ten Quiz

1. List the TAOS schools in 30 seconds or less. Hint: there are 10.

2. What are three ways to get your child into the college of your choice?
   a. A 4 plus grade average
   b. Build a Library
   c. Donate, Donate, Donate
   d. All of the above

ANSWER: D

3. What are the prerequisites for choosing a prep school?
   a. Expense
   b. Good Riding Stable
   c. Adorable Uniforms
   d. Scholastic Achievement
   e. All of the above

ANSWER: E

4. What is Miss Porter's and where is it located?
   a. Fine Girls School in Bethesda, Maryland
   b. Fine Girls School in Greenwich, Connecticut
   c. Fine Girls School in Peoria, Illinois
   d. Fine Girls School in Farmington, Connecticut

ANSWER: D – We didn't mention it previously. This is where research begins again. And while you are at it: Who is the most famous student to graduate from Miss Porter's? Hint: She is mentioned in our dedication.

5. What should concerned parents do to insure their children's acceptance to the college of choice?
    a. Hire an Ivy School Counselor
    b. Upload an audition tape to YouTube
    c. Have plans for a new campus library drawn up by a stellar architect
    d. Meet the President of the University with your attorney and check book

ANSWER: ALL BUT B.


6. What should you do if your dreams of a private education for your child are in jeopardy?
    a. Hire a Tutor immediately
    b. Look at student aid
    c. Call your well-heeled friends for letters of recommendation
    d. Get a second loan on your home
    e. A,B,C

ANSWER: E – Don't ever go to that extreme of getting a second loan on your home. The last thing you want is to be homeless if the economy tanks! You've worked too hard and too long!

(This page intentionally left blank)

# LESSON ELEVEN:
## Hobbies Worth your Worth

"Collection Mania"

COLLECTING HEIRLOOMS WHETHER in jewelry, watches, furniture, objet d'art, or coins can prove to be great fun and occasionally profitable if done correctly! Not only will some of these enhance your own person or home, they will simply provide one of the best reasons we can think of to travel the globe! There is always something on the other side of the world that you must at least take a look at for a prospective purchase. But you are saying now, "I just want to stay at home and relax occasionally." Not to worry, learn to play chess on your Royal Diamond Chess set. Such a lovely hobby and we know it will get the tongues wagging.

This little beauty was created by renowned French artist and jewelry master extraordinaire, Bernard Maquin and took over 4,500 hours to be created all by hand. When finished they used 1168.75 grams of 14 carat white gold, 9,900 black and white diamonds give or take, for a total weight of 189.09 carats. But the Brits, not to be outdone, have produced a set for over £5 million pounds, approximately $10 million dollars plus or minus for the exchange rate. Contact Boodles in England for pictures of this gold and platinum chess set replete with rubies, pearls, diamonds and emeralds. We feel sure that if you would prefer other stones that they will be happy to make your own personal set. Don't forget if you want to play Backgammon to relax by the pool or at night in front of the fireplace, a beautiful set including all of the necessary pieces to play has been created for the connoisseur that is covered with black, white and yellow diamonds. Please contact Charles Hollander for their latest works of art for games.

Alright, we hear you, total insanity to even think about owning these pieces, so check with Jacques in London for something more reasonable such as a limited edition Chess set made out of leather, brass and jet black ebony for approximately $5,550. O.K., still too much, just look for a chess set that is "not" made out of cardboard or plastic and start playing.

****

Continuing on to another topic for collections, let us address art. If you want original art, there are many famous artists such as Jamie Wyeth of Chadds Ford, Pennsylvania, or at the other extreme Andy Warhol, but there are also fresh new faces that need to be discovered. Now how does one know where to start? This is where being on all of those charitable boards can help. Let some of your well-heeled friends know that you are interested in supporting those "new and upcoming artists" in your home town. Possibly a stipend? Then become a bene-factor at your local museum and you will find out who is really going to increase in value down the road. Yes, those behind the scene deal-ers who help build museum collections should become your new best friends. Idle chit-chat between all can be most profitable.

We will add that if it seems to be too good to be true it probably is. Be very alert to dealers who are wholesalers. Guard your check-books carefully because your money could end up in Caribbean or a Swiss account. Second, when dealing with individuals that refuse to meet with you this is an instant RED FLAG , not a FLAUNT FLAG! They are merely trying to hype themselves by being reclusive and exclusive. Puh-leese, all you are going to do is pay more to purchase from them.

Now that you have been put on notice, we would recommend, if at all possible, to become a member of an influential coterie of individ-uals who would like to sponsor artists by putting on art shows. This is how the artists become famous but it is also a symbiotic relationship where you, too, become famous for supporting them. Rather ironic but that is another lesson in life to learn. Just think, you on the ground floor helping to make that new face and name a household word. And it all started with that first painting that you now have hanging in that special spot in the study, along with the rest of your collection.

Lastly, there is the easy way but the very expensive way to collect, just get out the check book and be prepared to spend millions and purchase a Monet or Picasso. Recently, Alice Walton, daughter of Sam Walton the founder of Wal-Mart fell into that category. Using her billions she has decided to build a museum called Crystal Bridges of American Art in Bentonville, Arkansas, to exhibit her collection. We are not kidding here, students. So you art afficienados from around the country are going to have to drive three hours from Kansas City to view this exhibit. It might not be Las Vegas where Steve Wynn, the casino mogul, has displayed his collection but it sure will put Bentonville on the map. Happy trails to all of you who decide to make the trip.

Remember in art if you want to be assured of authenticity you can start attending Sotheby's, Christie's, Doyle Bonham's and Butterfield's auctions to investigate art dealers. But most importantly, all art is personal and you should only be collecting art that speaks to you. Yes, you get up every morning in one of your homes and see that work hanging on the wall. Are you going to enjoy it for years to come? We hope so. Of course if it is really the "good stuff", students, and you tire of the picture then put it on the auction block. But we would hope that wouldn't be the case. Remember, think heirlooms for the family or helping to pay all of those college tuitions, too. Didn't we say you should always be planning for the future, students?

A small aside here: oils of the family are acceptable to hang on the walls and even pictures of the four-legged companions that have brought you fame and fortune. From your Westminster Best In Show Winner to your Derby Winner, it is fine to display them. (Please consult Lesson Sixteen for more information on Dog Showing.)

If you do "not" own that Best in Show canine beauty, dog art is still popular and does make for fine collectibles. Find a Cassius Marcellus

Cooldige, famed American dog painter, to hang on the wall. We don't want you to forget there is John Emms from England who specialized in dog oils and George Stubbs also from England whose pictures of horses are absolutely fabulous. Think of hanging dog or animal art work in your study or library. Very SOF! Unfortunately we must let you know that Mr's. Cooldige, Emms, and Stubbs are all deceased. So for painting your four-legged little or big beasties now, you will need to find a living modern day artist who specializes in dog or animal portraits. Call the Firestone's. We feel sure they could give you a name or two.

**\*\*\*\***

Proceeding along with collecting: gold coins should be authenticated by a reputable dealer. With a few discreet inquiries, you can usually find other SOF types who are personally collecting what you want or know someone who has fine credentials.

**Flaunt Flash News**: A rare 1913 U.S. Liberty Head nickel was recently sold for $3.7 million at public auction. Of course, there is always a good story connected to these sales. This coin is known as the Olsen-Hawn piece and is one of only five 1913 Liberty Head nickels known to exist. Two are currently in museums and three are privately held. Previous owners of the coin included Egypt's King Farouk and Jerry Buss, owner of the Los Angeles Lakers. A small aside here, students, remember in Lesson 4 we recommended buying real estate. How do you think that Jerry made all of his money? It wasn't buying and selling coins but then he only paid $200,000 for the coin in 1978 and we feel sure he didn't sell it for a loss. Jerry never sells anything for a loss. Kudos to another savvy businessman!

**\*\*\*\***

Now this is truly one of the more outlandish things we have heard of recently, so outlandish when it comes to collectibles we are almost at a loss for words. Winston Churchill's cigar "butt" sold in 2010 for $7,000. This was a half smoked cigar that he left after a meeting with his cabinet in 1941. It was saved by a servant and later given as a gift to a friend who passed it down to a family member. To validate that it belonged to Churchill, it still had his personalized label on it. So students, we are not sure if you really want to display this or just brag that you smoked Churchill's cigar while you drank a glass of port from 1941 with it. Your flaunt call on this one.

**FLAUNT FLASH FAILURE**: It has come to our attention recently that some of you might have turned into "hoarders." You have taken collecting and turned it into a nightmare. Yes your homes, garages, basements, barns and out buildings are overflowing with stuff. Stuff; a topic that the late comic George Carlin could do 15 minutes on. We won't elaborate on what he called your stuff, use your imagination!

You have become the laughing stock of the neighborhood! And to add insult to injury we understand that you want to appear on American Pickers. What is American Pickers? We had to ask the same question! It is a TV reality show where two men come to your home, pick through your things, or some might say your trash, and then offer you money on the spot for said items. Now, they might be nice guys, but this is not Antique Road Show.

This is not something to be proud of: either being a hoarder or appearing on a television reality show about trash. You might find your trash is so "picked over", that the pickers don't want it! If we should see you on American Pickers please do not tell them you have ever read our book! In fact, if you have a School of Flaunt graduation diploma, please return it ASAP. Your name will be removed from our graduation list!

****

If collecting is not your thing, then it is time to move onto hobbies. It is hard to determine when a collection becomes a hobby or vice versa, but lets consider starting a HORSE FARM! This is truly a hobby for the very rich! We at the School of Flaunt need a moment, please stop and let's have a few minutes of quiet for breeding does have so much breeding. This could be your new mantra.

How to start? So simple, the Keeneland yearling sales in Lexington, Kentucky, can easily get you on your way to a great stable! All the Saudis are doing this! Have you watched the Kentucky Derby lately? Trust us, this is mainly old time money at its finest. Don that stylish hat, ladies, and get ready to sip a Mint Julep. These are quite strong, so remember, no one "in their cups." Nothing worse than a slurring woman in a large hat!

Now lets discuss Kentucky, the land of "beautiful women, fast horses and good bourbon." Please note the farms in Lexington, Kentucky, have barns with mahogany lined stalls for their Derby winners. Mahogany is just not for people, students! And to complete that Flaunt Farm there are even gorgeous cemeteries with grand tombstones for their deceased equines who have brought them fame and fortune. (If this is out of the realm of possibilities for you please consult Lesson Sixteen, Our Pets, for more ideas.)

If you know nothing about these farms or horse flesh get thyself to the library and start boning up. Even though your goal is not to be an expert you should at the very least know the lingo. Remember these names: Calumet, Clairborne and Darby Dan. They are three of the oldest racing stables outside of Lexington in the Kentucky bluegrass. It is said that a crew of painters start at one end of the farm and it takes them one year to get back to their starting point. A never ending job but necessary!

Continuing on, as a small aside, do watch the Rose Bowl Parade. You question why? Because you will see some of the finest saddles decorated with silver on magnificent steeds. You just don't ride in the Rose Bowl, students, you are invited and you better have the right attire for the TV cameras to hone in on. Another hobby, collecting fine saddles.

Here is the epitome of hobbies: does your child have athletic talent and love horses? Dressage, Grand Prix hunter/jumper competition and going to Europe to buy that special horse and meet royalty aren't all that boring. Whether your fancy be watching your child compete, Point to Point racing, carriages, polo or thoroughbred racing they all require the big bucks to get the finest in horse flesh, equipment, training and jockeys.

Now we did mention Point to Point racing which is a Flaunt Fabulous hobby. If you don't know about it and you are going to be in the Wilmington, Delaware, area the first weekend of May, you surely don't want to miss this opportunity. First you will see some of the most wonderful carriages that will be paraded and then put on display for all to enjoy. Yes, the drivers and their guests are in their finest coaching outfits with their hounds present.

Secondly, you will also see some of the best tailgating ever! You will find our SOF devotees tailgating with crystal wine glasses, watching their horses raced over hill and dale, including jumps, only to receive some ribbons and points for future trophies. This is true Flaunt Flair and Fun at its best.

Call Winterthur Museum in Delaware for more details, but trust us the best parking spaces for tailgating and enjoying the spring breezes are reserved from year to year. You will have to get on someone's guest list or work your way up the reservation list for the best parking, when some unfortunate people drop out to get those spots! There is general admission (perish the thought,) so that you can wander around the rich and see how they like to tailgate. If nothing else, you can learn a few things. Wear your dark sunglasses and a hat for disguise if you do general admission. If you should run into someone you know an appropriate comment might be, "Oh, I was just in town to visit some friends in Philadelphia (remember never say Philly) and thought I'd pop over to see the races. We might be interested in this sport." Save some face, students, and hope that they invite you to their reserved tailgating area.

**\*\*\*\***

However, if horses are not fast enough company then start your own GRAND PRIX RACING TEAM! As in cars!!! One owner got into racing because his PR person spent $100,000 putting his company's logo on a car. When he saw that the logo was about 12" by 12" and the car was flying by at 200 mph he declared, "I want into this game. If people are paying this kind of money to have their company's name on a car I'm going to own one and let them pay for me to play." Play as in hobby! Note here: he had been collecting a garage full of cars from Lamborghinis to Porsches, what are a few more?

Remember half the fun with owning a race car is you can travel all over the world with this one. Parties, receptions, meeting and greeting of course are only going to enhance your reputation and possibly your pocket book. The race is fast and furious, especially in Europe, but ever so much fun! You will need a top team manager and lots of liquid cash, but lest you forget, we will remind you of our motto: MAKE IT BIG, FLAUNT IT BIG! Think Penske racing. Now is this a business or a hobby out of control?

**Flaunt Flash News**: Dario Franchitti wins the 2010 Indy 500. Celebrates with wife and well known actress, Ashley Judd. This makes our point for owning a racing team. You can party with the rich and famous and start new Flaunt Friendships today. A small aside here: Ashley is a Kappa Kappa Gamma and graduated from the University of Kentucky. Why do we bring this up? Life long friendships and good future connections are made through clubs, fraternities, sororities and common experiences. (Please review Lesson Ten and heed our advice well!)

****

Do you feel that some of these hobbies are just way over the top? O.K., we agree. Consider this, Mrs. Firestone allegedly spent over $100,000 per year campaigning one of her dogs to Best in Show at Westminster Kennel Club held in New York City. This is a very behind the scenes sport. You do nothing except write the checks and then proudly display your trophies. (Please consult Lesson Sixteen for more information on purchasing Show Dogs and Showing Etiquette.)

Now here is a fun hobby for a few hours. May we suggest that you take up Skeet shooting or Sporting Clays? Very politically correct because you aren't killing anything. If hunting doesn't bother you, go to Argentina and try Dove hunting. Of course, you will need your own custom firearm. Please be advised that a custom shotgun can take 16 months to sometimes 5 years to be built.

Know these names for superior makers of fine shotguns: Purdey, Boss and Woodward from England, Krieghoff from Germany and Ivo Fabbri, Beretta of Italy and last but not least Perazzi also from Italy. These lovely firearms have the finest engraving, woods and interchangeable stocks but get ready to spend approximately $10,000 for the low end, up to the high's possibly in the half a million dollar range. You always do get what you pay for! Before we forget do have a good safe to keep these pricey items in. We know of SOF types that like to have a room to display their treasures in but you are taking your chances. You have been warned! Security system up to date and working?

Continuing on: do you think you're finished with just having the shotgun, "no my pretty" you have just started. Sporting clays requires a cart to travel in at a shooting event. Why? Because the stations are so far apart and you might have to endure the heat. Simple remedy here, get ready to buy a small, air-conditioned, customized cart to haul you, a friend, your ammo and your firearms. Of course, how do you get this to the event? You need a trailer to put the cart on, then your Cadillac Escalade or Range Rover to haul everyone and everything in comfort. Whew, a lot of planning but like most things that are worth the time you must be ready to commit the buckos, too. Don't forget, have your estate Moniker put on the front of that cart, students.

**Note**: These carts can be rented at Sporting Clay competitions but isn't it just more fun to own your own cart and then use it to drive around your estate, too? Just a plan, students.

If you prefer only to be a collector of firearms, and please refer to them as firearms NOT guns or you will show that you are a real rookie, make sure you are on the list for auction house sales. Why? Because small hand-held firearms known as pistols, that have historical importance, e.g., owned by John Wilkes Booth, celebrities, or famous outlaws are always good buys if you can find them. Be careful when purchasing Civil War memorabilia though, some is really coveted and others are just nice to show off to friends and family.

****

Before we leave the topic of hobbies, remember we listed having a Croquet court on the grounds of your estate. Now this can be ever so much fun! Yes just a casual game for you and the family or serious cracking of the balls! From the Hamptons in NY to Beverly Hills, CA the rich and famous have been attacking those wooden balls and wickets since the early 1920s and 30s. Now this is a very fun hobby for you and the family.

You can also get very serious about this game and learn how to play competitively. Did you know that in competitive croquet the game needs to be completed in 90 minutes and there is even a 45 second shot clock to add extra pressure? This hobby could turn into a passion where your dream will be to win The Nationals and also beat the Brits at their own game.

But here is a little tip, do remember also that this back yard game can turn into a wonderful party. Set up two or more courts on your lawn. Give them the rules and watch the fun begin. Trust us, if you have set up the rules where they play three games and get points for placing, then the highest point makers are placed on the final team to compete for a lovely trophy you had made, their competitive juices will start to flow! We've had these amateur tournies and can only imagine what the games are like to win the Soloman Trophy, which is an annual tournament between America and England inaugurated in 1988. Let the Croquet begin!

Last for Flaunt Family Fun these hobbies always will be the tried and true: golf, tennis and snow skiing. All can bring you closer together and you have the added benefit of seeing some wonderful resorts in the process. Please take lots of lessons to become fairly proficient and not embarrass yourself or end up in the hospital! And just think, the little ones might actually turn out to be the next Gold medal winners at the Olympics, playing at Wimbledon, or on the Ryder Cup. Well, you can dream!

Should the children not turn out to be Olympians, not to worry, just buy your tickets and get ready. U.S. Open in NYC, here you come! Ski the great slopes of Europe and play golf, need we say, all over the world, and enjoy! Belong to the best clubs and remember, students, being seen at the right sporting venues is also part of SOF. (Please consult Lesson Seven for Vacations and Lesson Twelve on Being Seen.)

**Flaunt Fiscal Tip**: Take advantage of your Parks and School Sports Instruction. If you teach your children to "Play a Good Game," everyone will want to play with them!

# Lesson Eleven Quiz

1. Which of the following are not considered collectibles?
    a. Boehm Birds
    b. Cartier Gold Cuffs
    c. Rare Watches
    d. Kitchen Witches

ANSWER: D – Fairly obvious but what are Boehm Birds? Time for research students. Hint: one of our First Ladies of the land, as in married to a President, loved to collect them. She was also known for wearing red.

2. Can you name the impostor in this group of artists?
    a. JJ Petkus
    b. Jamie Wyeth
    c. Nick Africano

ANSWER: A

3. How much does a NBA Team cost?

    If you have to ask, you cannot afford one.

4. What's the most important thing behind an NFL Team?
    a. The Brains
    b. The Brawn
    c. The Uniforms
    d. Money
    e. All of the Above

ANSWER: E

5. Which of the following is not a true SOF endorsed pastime?
    a. Skeet Shooting
    b. Attending "Art Basel" in Miami
    c. Fly Fishing with a Guide
    d. Attending the Equestrian Olympic Trials
    e. Dirt Biking

ANSWER: F – Let us be Crystal Clear students, … NO DIRT BIKING.

6. Why pay $2,000,000 at the Keeneland yearling sale for a colt?
    a. Money is no object for a blue blood
    b. You probably have a potential Triple Crown Winner
    c. Syndication when the colt is three will probably be worth $10,000,000
    d. To get your picture in the August issue of Town and Country magazine
    e. All of the above

Answer: E

7. Why is Collecting Mania the rage?
    a. Determined collectors bidding
    b. Rarity
    c. Cocktail conversation
    d. True SOF Flaunt!
    e. All of the above

ANSWER: E – With the newly rich in China and the rest of the world you can only expect the prices of rare objects to continue to climb!

## LESSON TWELVE:
## Sporting Events
"See and Be Seen or Participate"

LET'S GET RIGHT to the point here students. You've worked long and hard to get to the top, or you have won the Mega Millions. Now that you are there, you can either be seen or participate in the sport of your choice. Being seen obviously is the easiest way to go since you simply provide the capital. Others provide the brawn and bravado. We will discuss participation later in this lesson.

Note: Mark Cuban, owner of the Dallas Mavericks, loves being part of the bravado! We do enjoy his enthusiasm courtside. But we digress, let us continue ...

In some of our other lessons we went into details about hobbies that could lead to the spotlights of TV cameras and print. We decided that more elaboration was needed on how to handle these new situations because you are now a mini-celebrity in your own right.

Please remember if you are attending an event only the very best seats will do students. If you own the team that is a given! But if you don't then a Sky Box whenever available would provide adequate seating! This goes both for sporting and top entertainment. Nothing like the Stones from your private sky box or taking the children to see their favorite rock star too! Much safer than having to deal with all of those crazy fans below you. But lets not talk about the masses here.

We want to discuss either you being seen at a sporting event or actually participating. Both of which can be great fun!

Now, half the enjoyment in going to an event is being seen and seeing who else is there. We have recommended the Sky Box which you will have to pay a large price for but it will be well worth it. People will notice when you are entering your Sky Box, and as a result many will ask for your autograph, because they will assume you must be someone to be sitting in such a regal space! Be pleasant about it and humor them, then explain you just never make it a habit! (Please consult Lesson Six on Attitude and Manners.) Remember donate your box for charity auctions. This is a total win-win for everyone involved and your accountant will love you too.

****

But the topic here is being seen or participating. So let's continue with being seen. As we previously mentioned, the greatest thrill of all, if you are a great sports fan and really have money to blow, is owning a Formula One race team (being seen) or possibly riding your own Polo ponies (participating) as in playing Polo with the Duke of Cambridge when he is visiting here in the States. Both totally chic, certainmont, (remember your French, students). Now we are talking total flaunt!

**Note**: If you are concerned about passing on your heirlooms too soon, hire someone to race those cars for you. Think Bobby Rahal and David Letterman. No dummies there. They also found Danica Patrick! Bingo a sports sensation and they recoup all the glory. OK, so now she drives for another company … her loss, n'est-ce pas?

**Flaunt Flash News**: Danica is now driving NASCAR. Looks like a major win for Go Daddy! We have to admit that we love the fact that she can compete with the boys.

But let's get back to the topic of being seen. Racing is a great way to be "seen" as the TV cameras pan to you the owner talking with your driver before the race. As a small aside, plan on arriving in your mega-expensive motor home with your friends, and then wander around in the infield during the time trials or the actual race. It is so much fun to either be in the pit area as an owner, or just to have your family hanging out while sitting on top of that motor home. Trust us, these can be the best seats at the track. Plus you never have to stand in line for one of those terrible public restrooms! Your motor home is worth it just for that reason alone.

Not enough limelight for you with owning polo ponies or race cars? Do you prefer being in the mega-limelight? We suggest then purchasing an NFL, NBA or major league baseball team. Soccer is hot now, too, and probably a lot more reasonable for team purchase, unless you are thinking of overseas. Picture you in the latest issue of Sports Illustrated being interviewed or better yet on television or radio. All go hand in hand with ownership! Don't forget all of those cameras zooming in on your Sky Box as you high five the wife after a score!

Note: Please make sure that it is spelled out in black and white who owns the team. Think LA Dodgers. That was a nasty one!

So your city doesn't have a team, never fear, start lobbying the "local politico" to build the stadium but remember you get the big tax write-offs for years to come also. Naturally this will catapult your family into as much fame as being a Founding Father or even playing on said team. Let's face it students, it is so much fun to be in the glow of a Super Bowl Championship or winning the World Series! You the owner standing on the podium lifting and waving the trophy! Then thanking everyone for making this possible. How much fun was that? LOTS! A little aside, you will be exhausted after said win, but your jet should be ready to whisk you off to a relaxing respite. Being seen can be so exhausting!

Okay, okay, we can now hear you saying, "I can't afford to buy a team!" Not to worry, can your business use a tax write-off for entertaining? YES is the correct answer. Well, get that sky box and enjoy those games. You can have them catered, replete with your own open bar and "dessert cart" wheeled in for your guests. We personally "enjoy" that dessert cart and please do invite your Divas of Good Taste, Alexandra and Cate! But lets continue ... remember, students, and this is so important, hire buses to bring your guests. They can imbibe and enjoy!

Please stop your whining about not wanting to purchase a sky box. We are getting a splitting headache from listening to this dribble. Just buy the court side tickets, seats at the 50 yard line or behind home plate. Yes the rich and famous do sit there also. We know you have seen Jack Nicholson court side. You never can tell when you can strike up a new friendship and where that can lead!

****

Now let's continue on to participating! As we told you in Lesson Eleven on hobbies, we do want you to learn at least one sport "well" enough to participate. Whether that be skiing (not water), tennis, golf, shooting skeet or the newest hot shooting sport called Sporting Clays, do it well. Why? Remember, you are a mini-celebrity now and if the Paparazzi are hiding behind that bush to take your picture, you should be playing well and looking great! God forbid that you end up on TMZ looking horrid! Picture you in the snow with your skis planted over your head and your derriere showing! Ladies, this is why we say no tramp stamps or tattoos. One might as well consider going into hiding for some time after that gets broadcast around the world! If you have made the mistake of getting one of those huge ghastly tattoos on your back and derriere you probably are stuck with it. (Although, we advise that you seek the help of a great Plastic Surgeon for immediate removal. See Lesson Fourteen on Plastic Surgery.) Think long and hard before you pay money for these "tacky tats!" We give no SOF seal of approval on tramp stamps, etc., … !

Now, as for those pesky reporters with their audio cameras, never and we repeat, never lose your cool! How awful for the world to see you shoving a reporter or throwing his camera to the ground, let alone swearing. Consult Lesson Six again to refresh your memory on the difference between the cool stare and the cold stare that we have recommended for such situations and please, again "no" swearing. It is absolutely forbidden. So suck it up; you are rich and famous now! This probably might be a good time to just flash them that million-dollar smile (we know you have gotten one from your Park Avenue DDS) and give them a thumbs up.

Remember we said you want to be able to participate in at least one of these sports, but know something about all of them; that way you can enjoy those flaunt conversations. Just sitting like a bump on a log while everyone else is bantering about ski slopes, handicaps or the U.S. Open makes you a dull dinner guest!

Note: Talking about bowling tournaments, unless they were for your children on your home alley, and tossing around the horseshoes are verboten—that's German for tacky. We have nothing against horseshoes mind you, but hide those pits behind the hedges! We have never seen one that is pretty. But we digress again, back to being seen and participating.

Conversations, TALK A GOOD GAME! Talking a good game is almost as important as playing but our preference obviously is for you to play well! Think about this, you playing at the Bob Hope Pro-Am golf tournament in Palm Desert with the pros and celebrities. TV cameras zeroing in on you putting and high-fiving with your pro. Now that is being seen and participating.

Students, at the very least, as a good golfer so appropriately put it, "dress like you shoot in the 70s, talk like you shoot in the 80s and get away with shooting in the 90s." Please at the worst the low 90s! You are bordering on being a duffer now. Reputation, alas you have a reputation to keep up. And remember everyone has a camera phone now. Think YOU TUBE and you playing poorly! Enough said. Lastly, don't forget the right outfit. Golf chic goes in and out of style so be sure to check out the pro shop for the current trends.

Lest we forget, a true SOF plum would be owning a Garia Cart! The world's most expensive golf cart! Now that would get the old boys' tongues wagging on the links. Ah, they are now all looking! We do love being seen. (Please consult Lesson Eleven for more information on Hobbies Worth Your Worth.)

****

This brings us to getting to the event. How do you want the public to see you? As we spoke about earlier, motor homes are acceptable for this because you can party to and from. Remember, always hire a driver. The host would like to party too. If the event is out of town, have your pilot and jet ready to whisk you off and have a limo ready at your destination! Or at least charter a plane. Remember SOF devotees do not like lines. Our mantra, NO LINES EVER! Repeat that three times to yourself now for this is an achievable goal, students. NO LINES EVER, NO LINES EVER, NO LINES EVER. Oh, we feel better immediately!

****

Lastly, SOF does not in any way advocate the illegal, but we are not blind either! BET, BET, BET! WIN, WIN, WIN! We are not talking the two dollar window, students. Football pools are fun, but let's face fact, your local bookie or Las Vegas contacts can be known as man's best friends! This does add some gusto to watching that game! And possibly being seen with your local Bookie might not be a good idea! Needless to say, don't lose your shirt, your Rolex and/or the family estate. My God, it would be so tacky to have to dip into the little one's trust funds. Enough said, now go have a good time!

# Lesson Twelve Quiz

1. What is a chucker?
    a. Rotten fruit you should throw out
    b. A short strand of rare pearls
    c. A period of polo play

ANSWER: C – We did not discuss this term but this is why you always need to be doing research so you are not the dullard in the group.

2. List Five NFL owners you have recently lunched with:

Just trying to keep you on your toes! Can you list one owner of any major sporting team that you can have lunched with? No can do? Then you are definitely not trying to be SOF material.

3. What are the two rules of good gamesmanship?
    a. Lying and Cheating
    b. Abusive language and gestures
    c. Dress and talk a good game

ANSWER: C

4. How do you get to a sporting event?
    a. Grey Hound Bus
    b. Private Jet
    c. Chauffeured Motor Home
    d. Sub Compact
    e. B & C

ANSWER: E

5. Which German Phrase for "TACKY" was used in Lesson 8?
    a. Danka
    b. Bitte
    c. Verboten
    d. Schwarztkoff

ANSWER: C – And please practice French Phrases in Lesson Six. THERE WILL BE A QUIZ!

6. What is a Tramp Stamp?
    a. USPS tribute to Red Skelton
    b. Areas where Hobos catch a box car or gather round a roaring fire
    c. Disgusting tattoo on the lower part of one's back
    d. Universal Mark of the Tacky and Tasteless
    e. C & D

ANSWER: E

(This page intentionally left blank)

The Elms

The Elms

# LESSON THIRTEEN:
## Names, Titles, and Monikers

"What's on Your Stationary?"

SURNAMES ARE SO important. A fine family name carries weight and packs a punch! Should your family name lack luster there are alternatives …

Dress it up a bit or add to it! Hyphenated names, long the pinnacle of British High Society can be yours. Get out the phone book and be creative. Cultivate a wonderful new lineage. If all seems hopeless, then you might consider changing your name. (See your attorney to make this legal.) If you are female, this can be arranged through marriage. Note we did not say, "Duh."

Speaking of marriage, it can do many things for those wise enough to do it well! Emotionally and financially merging fortunes is so rewarding.

Don't Rule out Royalty! Have a family tree done and if there are no royals to speak of in your lineage, then alas you might have to marry into it yourself, or at least have one of your children marry into a Royal Family. Hello Kate Middleton!

Think Lord or Duke, Countess or Lady, for it means a first class ticket to the society pages! And of course all your best friends will be royalty as well!

A curious thing about those titled faces one sees in the society columns: Doesn't it seem that anyone giving a large bash in Europe has a prefix to his or her name? Lord and Lady This, Prince von Something of That. We delved deeper and found these titles are not only loosely passed down, they are BOUGHT AND SOLD!

Titles and Knighthoods are yearly passed out by the Queen of England, provided one has proven oneself worthy of said honor. A significant contribution to national life is a criterion for receiving the title of Sir. Interesting … Sir Elton John, Sir Paul McCartney, etc. Could this be because they are rich? We are curious. One does not know what goes on behind closed doors at the palace. Let's just put it this way, if you have to ask how much, you cannot afford it. Sometimes an easier way to receive a title is with titled land that is auctioned off regularly. Consult London's finest Auction Houses for further information.

Just think, Lord of the Manor from Davenport, Iowa! My, my you have arrived! Where there is a will there is always a way, your highness.

A few such titles for your perusal: Duke, Duchess, Lord, Lady, Count, Countess, and of course, Prince and Princess. The pinnacle titles of King and Queen take generations usually to achieve. Unless you purchase your own island and then why not just proclaim your-selves to be the King and Queen of Blah, Blah, land. Stop laughing; there will be someone who does that!

Just a short word on first names, students. Celebrities seem hell-bent on naming their offspring after Fruits, Vegetables and Biblical Heroes who part Seas. Don't do this … Your children will hate you! If one nicknames one's child after a fruit, so be it. See, we can be rea-sonable and we do love a Peachy or a Plum! Flowers may be acceptable as in Lily, Rose or Violet, but not much more as in Hyacinth. Strong sophisticated names will serve you well and ensure a better stab at a Presidential run. We know of no CEOs named: Apple. Only Laptops … wait that didn't sound right. End of discussion.

## Lesson Thirteen Quiz

1. Which of the following are acceptable boy's names?
    a. Little Moses
    b. Little Bradley
    c. Little Herbert
    d. Little Palmer
    e. B & D
    f. A & B

ANSWER: E

2. Which of the following are acceptable girl's names?
    a. Little Katherine
    b. Little Paris
    c. Little Stephanie
    d. Little Apple
    e. Little Nini
    f. A, B & C

ANSWER: F – Little Nini, you can't be serious, you really didn't choose that one!

3. Which title would your rather acquire through marriage?

   Don't quibble, just get one!

4. If your family tree is unhealthy, where do you start pruning?

Disavow any knowledge of mud wrestling champions, dirt bike racers and anyone who has ever been called a Good Ol' Boy in your family!

5. What/Who are Honorables?
   a. Award winning authors
   b. Younger children of Titled British.
   c. Winning pies at the Wisconsin State Fair
   d. Those coming in beyond Bronze in the Olympics

ANSWER: B


6. Would the middle name of BOB be appropriate in any circumstance? e.g., Jim Bob, Ray Bob, Billy Bob …

ANSWER: NEVER EVER! Are they still doing that south of the Mason Dixon line?

(This page intentionally left blank)

# LESSON FOURTEEN:
## Plastic Surgery
"A Stitch in Time Saves Nine—Years That is"

ONE OF THE most serious of SOF endorsements goes to those dedicated surgeons of the Plastic variety! Why pray for miracles when you need only make an appointment?

"Oh, that this too solid flesh would melt?" Well, trust us, it can! Bob it, tuck it, lift it, but do it! Put your best face and frame forward. Plus, in a number of cases your health might be improved by any of these techniques. Well, that might be stretching the point, but you surely will be getting a much needed psychological boost and feel so much better when you look in the mirror. Isn't that half the battle?

No more getting up in the morning and thinking, "the good, the bad and the ugly!" Forget that bulbous nose, lack of bootie or boob issues. All can be improved. But please remember that you will always need to return for a little upkeep and that is why you have doctors. Sorry if you have no ankles, bowed or bottle legs; our only suggestion is try to cover them up. Doctors can only go so far. Little ones' bowed legs and toed-out feet should be corrected at a very early age.

Let's just get this question settled now because we know it is one of the first things you Ladies think about. What, you ask? The old question of when is too much too much? You know what we are talking about: breasts!

The answer is simple. When your breast size looks like you should be working on your next pole dance routine or possible porn film, that is too much!

Please, Ladies, we know the temptation is there. You've always felt that you were, shall we say, flat. We are begging you, don't go overboard. Speaking of overboard, such as falling off the boat into the water, when your breasts look like floaties you have definitely gone too far. Let's think about this, do you really only want people to be looking at your breasts and not at your face, after you just spent all of that time and money to make sure you look fabulous? We hope the answer is no and you will practice some restraint with the implants.

Now speaking of implants, they can "wander!" Yes, Students, implants can take on a life of their own … moving hither and yon and you cannot stop them. They know it and will try to get away at any cost! Also they can contract "folds," as in implant folds. Never heard of them? Well, they do exist and let us tell you, they are not pretty.

No plastic breast surgeon is going to give you all these dirty little implant secrets! So be forewarned. Oops, one more little problem … deflation. Yes, you heard it right. They POP! They LEAK! They slowly die a silent death. One day you are in the shower and you think you have lost your mind … why am I so lopsided? Back to the surgery ward but quick! We won't go any further because we think you have the picture now. Before we forget, if you have the opposite problem of too much, then please get those breasts reduced. Your back will thank you for it and you will look so much better in your clothes. Remember gravity, Ladies. You can't stop it!

As for facial surgeries, you don't want to end up looking like a "cat woman." You have all seen someone like this before. They look like the Cheshire Cat. Their face is pulled back so tight, they are in a permanent state of smiling. Their eyes really have no upper lids left and the eyebrows are next to the hair line. We can only advise you to be responsible and know when enough is enough! If you can't exhibit restraint, and keep going from Doctor to Doctor and they all are refusing to do anymore surgery, then trust us you have reached the point of enough! Call a psychiatrist, instead.

**\*\*\*\***

Which leads us to using Botox. Yes, it can be wonderful, but also be very, very careful. We had neighbors that always looked so unpleasant, both husband and wife. Naturally we never made any effort to meet them. Well, we came to find out that they both got Botox on a regular basis. It was impossible for them to smile! They were permanently in a state of being facially frozen. Students, how do you ever think you will be on the "A" list for parties if you can't even smile? We see "B" list written all over your frozen face! Very, very bad!

**Note**: In Lesson Five we spoke about parties "not" to have. Well surprise, surprise, students, we learned this couple used to have Botox parties. Their skin also had that shiny plastic look . Possibly one too many peels? Just a thought.

**\*\*\*\***

Alas, you or your husband has had plastic surgery and the little ones resemble your former self. Fear not, after sixteen those noses can be corrected just like you did. Why should any young person not avail themselves of being able to improve upon Mother Nature and heredity? Never let little juniors of either sex go through life with unpleasant features, such as crooked teeth and trophy ears. These are easily taken care of. Actually we knew of many a high school student that not only got their nose done but had their ears pinned back at the same time. It was called a Happy 16th Birthday present. True, we don't make these things up! Mommy and Daddy threw in a new car, too, because they were so worried about little Junior's self esteem, but then that is another topic.

Of course, we at the School of Flaunt do not endorse breast augmentation for anyone under twenty one years of age. Besides, in many cases, it makes one look "heavy." And whatever you do, do not, we repeat, do not succumb to the pouty lip augmentation!!! Do you really think that looking like an Angel fish with blown-up lips is some how going to make you look sexy? Ghastly that one … total Flaunt Failure!

Remember here, students, you are not trying to look like Barbie, you are merely trying to just improve your image. Someone should have told a reality star who will remain nameless that! Talk about overboard Barbie! Puh-leese!

Ladies and gentlemen, lets face facts here, a stitch in time does save at least 9 years. Another true story: we recently saw an old friend who had shed 60 pounds, not kidding you, and had a neck lift and eyes done. She really did look 9 years younger. We wouldn't lie to you, students. It could only be described as a dramatic change. Stunning! She was Flaunt Fabulous! That could be you too.

Now if you really want to go for the full makeover then look into a face lift, for it can set back that clock big time. Just remember that you are a good candidate if your skin still has some elasticity and you also have a well defined bone structure. You can also have a forehead lift and your eyelids done at the same time. Sounds like a lot of surgery so please only get the best plastic surgeon! ONLY BOARD CERTIFIED should touch you and in an Accredited Surgery Center!! As a small aside for those of you who prefer not to have general anesthesia, you "may" be able to have this procedure done with local anesthesia combined with a sedative to make you drowsy and relaxed.

Do your research students and select only the most reputable physicians with the highest of recommendations. If at all possible, find a local nurse to tell you all. They know who is the best!

During your consultation with both doctor and anesthesiologist, please discuss every detail of your operation and recovery. Have plenty of staff and a good nurse to cover for you, as you recoup at the nearest 5 Star Hotel or your Club. Large hat and sunglasses and you are even good to take a walk around the block! One maid we know in a posh New York Women's Club regularly advises the guests who have had recent surgery and are staying a few days out of sight. She is invaluable and the tips prove it!

STUDENTS, if you have been under a rock and do not know the latest in surgical adventures, here are a few:

Rhinoplasty
Smile Makeover
Tummy Tuck
Chin Implant
Eye Lift
Full Face Lift
Dermabrasion
Laser Treatments
Chemical Peels
Blue Light for Acne
Ear Bob
Breast Reduction
Breast Augmentation
Facial Rejuvenation
Cosmetic Breast Surgery
Body Contouring/Liposuction
Laser Liposuction/Cool Lipo
Labiaplasty
Breast Reconstruction after Cancer Surgery
Spider Veins, Varicose Veins and Broken Vessels Removal

**\*\*\*\***

So you are looking for something a little less invasive ...

What is the new Cool Lipo?

As we grow older our skin begins to show the signs of sun, life-style, and aging. The face and neck are exposed to the sun more than any other part of the body; therefore, they both tend to age more quickly. As these aging effects begin to appear we look for topical formulas and non-invasive treatments to help reduce future aging, plus improve current appearance. Many prefer not to undergo extensive surgical face and neck lifts due to the expense and risk. Additionally, these procedures require significant time for the face and neck to heal, not always an option for people with limited recovery time.

What to do? Don't fret; there is now Cool Lipo (laser-assisted lipolysis) which is a new, minimally invasive technology that freezes fat cells for easy removal. It is a laser-based procedure that breaks up and removes fat cells in areas such as under the chin, neck, and jowls or areas with loose skin such as the arms. In addition, the unique wave length of the Cool Lipo laser system directly contracts collagen and tightens the skin, an effect not seen with standard liposuction. OH STUDENTS!! THIS IS AMAZING!!! GOODBYE LOVE HANDLES!

Take a look at the Benefits:
    Gentle fat disruption and removal technique for small areas
    Treats areas that are difficult for conventional liposuction
    Less invasive than a neck or face lift
    May be performed under local anesthesia only
    Short procedure in your physician's office
    Safe with minimal bruising and side effects
    Minimal downtime post-procedure

****

O.K. students, now you have focused on your body and face but did you know that your hands can give your age away? Think of those hands that show off those large bulbous veins, age spots and have that crocodile dry skin look. Horrors! Not on our students! Whether you are 30 or 70 there is still hope for you. It is called hand rejuvenation. Costs run from a mere $500 up to $2,000 depending on the damage and aging that needs help.

For those of you who only need to take care of some dull and rough skin think microdermabrasion. It is a totally painless exfoliating treatment that gets rid of dead surface cells and at the same time stimulates new cell growth with a series of treatments. May we remind you, please always follow up with "maintenance" and you'll have hands that a model would be jealous of.

Oh, so you have some ugly little dark spots along with drab color on your hands. Then you should consider a slightly more aggressive solution, chemical peels! Inquire about a Vi Peel, TCA or Jessners and always remember that these should be performed by a medical esthetician or physician. Then there is always Intense Pulse Light Laser Therapy that can eliminate damaged skin from too much sun. Unfortunately, all of these treatments do require more than one visit. So if time is of the essence "think one" treatment. It can be so simple, students. Go for Laser Resurfacing. Voila, immediately those signs of sun exposure, accidental scars and that unsightly evidence of aging are gone!

If your hands are looking thin and lack volume you absolutely need to consider injectables. Juvederm, Restylane or Radiesse can give your hands that young, plump and supple look again. Fillers work for your hands as well as your face, students! Remember, as we always recommend, do your homework, meet your doctor and then select the treatment that is best for you. Aren't you the sexy girl or guy now?

Lastly, if you think that your hands don't matter we must tell you a true story. Alexandra as you all know was a flight attendant. When she was serving drinks she handed one of her passengers a beverage. She almost dropped it into her lap as her eyes darted back and forth between the face and the hands. She couldn't help herself. Why? Well, this woman looked fantastic. Great clothes, jewelry and beautiful face. But her hands! They were the hands of an older woman. Alexandra was stunned to put it mildly. Students of Flaunt, don't forget your hands! They do tell the whole story. Alexandra did refrain from asking her who her surgeon was, even though she was dying to know!

Everything that we have talked about above can be done for our SOF men too, with the exception of Breast Augmentation, or maybe that is called Pec augmentation? Sorry guys but those pecs and six packs only come with hours of hard work in the gym. Remember, we ladies also like a little eye-candy, so start lifting those weights! Man boobs can be removed by your plastic surgeon.

Gas up the car or fuel the plane, get out on the road today and research those Doctors. Beauty is only a personal check away. Remember though if your family is telling you to stop having procedures then you should put that check or credit card away.

**Flaunt Fiscal Tip**: Consult with your Dr. about his payment plan. Check with your local Credit Union or Bank for personal loans. Note: never jeopardize your home with a home equity line of credit. You might have a great face, but nowhere to live.

# Lesson Fourteen Quiz

1. What areas of the body can be enhanced with Liposuction?
   a. Chin
   b. Thighs
   c. Buttocks
   d. Arms
   e. Waist
   f. Ankles
   g. All of the above and more ...

ANSWER: G


2. Where do you find a good Plastic Surgeon?
   a. Recommendations from your personal physician
   b. Articles in Town and Country
   c. The "Ugly Duckling" Reality Show
   d. Top Medical Centers
   e. A nurse *
   f. A, D, & E

ANSWER: F


*Good Nurses are invaluable in finding a great surgeon. They see everything that goes on in the offices and surgical wards. Listen to their words of wisdom ... also plan to have a nurse care for you after your surgery. There is nothing worse than a blood-shy cleaning lady or maid who cannot bear to look at you in your bandages. Many a maid has fainted at the sight of a bandaged, seeping, plastic surgery patient ... what good would that do? Remember cell phone cameras too. One does not want TMZ and the gossip rags telling all about your surgeries. Only people who have a signed a non disclosure should have contact with you directly after surgery. You will thank us later for this tidbit!

3. How is a Smile Makeover Different than Orthodontia? Please answer in 30 words or less.

4. If Junior has a problem with blemishes, what is a great new treatment?
    a. Red Light Special at Wal Mart
    b. Clearasil
    c. Female Hormone Treatment
    d. Blue Light Treatment

ANSWER: D

5. Who should consider Breast Augmentation?
    a. Anyone over the age of 25 that REALLY needs it
    b. Only Strippers and Chorus Girls
    c. Reality Stars of Housewives of Wherever …
    d. National News Anchors

ANSWER: A

6. Which of the following celebrities has NOT had Plastic Surgery?
    a. Pamela Anderson
    b. Cher
    c. Taylor Swift
    d. Michael Jackson
    e. Heidi Montag

ANSWER: C – If anyone answered Heidi Montag or Michael Jackson, please return this book and confess to the proprietor that you are an idiot.

7. Should you have your hands done before or after a facelift?
    a. Before
    b. After
    c. We don't care just have them done if they need it!

ANSWER: C

## LESSON FIFTEEN:
## Amour or Affair de Coeure …
### "We want to Light Your Fire"

IN MODERN-DAY SOCIETY, no book is complete without a lesson on sex, and alas, violence. We suggest that you have plenty of the former and none of the latter and you'll be fine. With all of the health problems today, please be discriminating in the choosing of a love interest. Remember human bondage, black leather, (other than car interiors), and whips are not SOF endorsements.

Your DVD collection and Internet wanderings might rival Playboy Magazine; of course these are all very personal areas and as long as you are not sadistic and your partner enjoys such things, we cannot comment on what goes on behind closed doors. Just remember, "Do you want to be caught dead in this situation?" Many a philanderer has kicked the bucket with his Trophy girlfriend or her Boy Toy in a not-so-dignified manner. Be forewarned and check those Blood Pressure Meds! We know of one widower who had a hard time finding his Hollywood Diva Wife's Bentley, so secretive were the paramedics and police who came upon this poor woman's demise and her "Boy Toy" wasn't talking …

Now, speaking of do you want to be caught dead in certain situations? Corresponding has taken on a totally new meaning. What, pray tell, are we referring to? Sexting! Yes, we aren't talking Pen Pals here! Sexting, as we are sure you all must know, unless you are living under a rock, is doing the nasty on your cell phone with pictures and text speak. And there are even cyberspace rules. Who knew? Well now you do.

Here are the Cyberspace rules:

1. Don't sext if you think it will be unwelcome. What? We can see you rolling your eyes now, we did too!
2. If you haven't been to bed together it might be a bad idea. Do you think?
3. Descriptions work better than images for most women. No comment!

Listen up, students. You are not a "wanna be" celebrity, passé Movie star or a sports celebrity who thinks they can get away with this stupid behavior. Pictures of your privates whether sent by texting or taken by the Paparazzi, as you get in and out of a car, will be splashed across the tabloids and are going to be out there forever! Once it is on the internet, always on the internet.

Do you really want to have to stand in front of the press and say your mea culpa, "I'm sorry," over and over and over again ad nauseam? Better learn to cry with lots of tears; picture a Jimmy Swaggart moment, you with your tissues begging for forgiveness. Puh-leese, all because you had to send a sexually explicit picture or text. Trust us we have no sympathy for this poor behavior and if you are on a board or President of a Fortune 500 company they won't either!

Here are our sexting rules: DO NOT SEND sexually explicit comments or pictures over your cell phone, by e-mail, leave on a message machine or even send by snail mail! NEVER EVER! Capisce?

Take care of your relationships, students; here is a story of one of the dimmer bulbs on the planet:

*A husband and wife go to a counselor after 16 years of marriage. The counselor asks them what the problem is and the wife goes into a tirade, listing every problem they have ever had in the 16 years they've been married. She goes on and on and on.*

*Finally, the counselor gets up, walks around the desk, embraces the wife and kisses her passionately.*

*The woman shuts up and sits quietly in a daze.*

*The counselor turns to the husband and says, "This is what your wife needs at least three times a week. Can you do this?"*

*The husband thinks for a moment and replies, "Well, I can drop her off here on Mondays and Wednesdays, but on Fridays, I play golf."*

You giggle but sadly many a relationship is in this sorry state. You, who live life to the fullest, owe it to yourself and your spouse to live, love and nurture. Read the following before it is too late:

SOF always recognizes the best champagnes and a dip in the Jacuzzi with your partner. Plenty of wonderful French or Italian milled soaps, oils and bubble baths are a must.

Votive candles placed throughout the bath and bedroom are wonderful for those romantic evenings or "getaways" with that special person. Aromatherapy candles are also lovely and there are so many scents to choose from: Pomegranate, Lavender, Lilac and Jasmine. Ooh, la, la! Makes you want to pop the champagne and take an olive oil bath.

Please make sure that those lit candles are never near said bed of pleasure. We only want to light your fire not set the room on fire. Picture the headlines in your local paper: Five Alarm Fire at The Elms! Underneath is a "picture" of you and your significant other standing in front of your home, wrapped up in blankets, with your million dollar sex toy in hand. HUMILIATING!!

Note: Sex toys will be discussed later in this lesson. No cheating now, you cannot start scanning to get to that part of the lesson.

But getting back to pictures in the paper, if you think that won't happen remember everyone and their Grandmother now has their cell phone at the ready to take pictures. Or better yet, TV News Helicopters doing fly-bys! This means you will be on the morning, afternoon and evening news too! Will it be picked up by the national news companies, e.g., CNN, FOX etc.? Probably! So just remember to practice "safe" sex in every way, Students!

Continuing on, always wear expensive silk lingerie and don't forget the Egyptian cotton sheets and feather pillows that can add that sensuous touch! And speaking of lingerie we do not put our seal of approval on edible underwear but if this is your thing please do not tell your partner that we recommended it! Heaven forbid that we put added pressure on your relationship. Possibly instead you might keep some chocolate bon bons near by for you and "whoever." Yummy!

**Flaunt Flash News**: The robe for the woman who has everything just came on the market. A stunning creation of an ankle length 100% pure cashmere robe with a genuine fox collar. Retail approximately $750. For those who prefer non-fur, a 100% pure cashmere ankle length robe is also available for $450. Now that is something to snuggle up in, in front the fireplace on a cold evening, with your loved one. Get out the cognac, students!

****

How to decorate that boudoir should go to the top of your priorities now. First of all remember these names, Pratesi and Anichini. Pratesi is an Italian company that was founded in 1896 that produces only the highest in quality linens. From heads of state to royalty, CEO's of Fortune 500 companies and celebrities they all want Pratesi on their beds. Each piece takes approximately two years from beginning to end before it will be available for purchase. They use only the finest in southern Egyptian cotton and each piece is hand embroidered by an artisan. Even if you can't afford Pratesi at the very least remember this, Three Lines. It is one of their classic designs! Lastly, they also do have table linens and beach wear accessories. Heaven forbid that you be seen pool side without a Pratesi bag to carry that sun block in. Just a thought, students.

Now who is Susan Dollenmaier? She is the CEO and founder of Anichini. This is a high-end manufacturer of bed linens, table linens, decorative accessories, e.g., pillows to die for, merino wool throws and fabric by the yard. Ms. Dollenmaier produces items that will be your antiques of tomorrow. Her products can only be described as sensuous, beautiful and detailed with old world craftsmanship. If you enter a store that carries her products we will almost guarantee that you will start salivating in excitement and not know where to even start looking. Calm yourself and get ready to spend hours exploring!

**Flaunt Fiscal Tip**: More good news for you students. There is actually an Anichini "outlet" store in New Lebanon, NH. Oh we kid you not! If you are ever in Boston this is definitely worth the drive. Be prepared to spend at least 2 hours in that Mecca of beauty! Ha, that is a short time. We at SOF have easily spent 3 hours shopping there.

**Flaunt Flash News**: The Anichini store has opened in West Hollywood! We understand that Cher loves Anichini too. Cher has been described as a long-time Anichini aficionado. Working with her designer, Martyn Lawrence-Bullard, Cher used the muga silk collection in abundance in her bedroom. Think natural golden luminescence. Knowing that our Diva Cher is always up on the very best of everything and that we at the School of Flaunt love Anichini, too, who could ask for better recommendations!

Sorry you aren't in New Hampshire or California, well then you just need to consult with your designers. But do not be depressed, there are also many other lovely linen manufacturers and designers. Watch for those sales if possible and remember, you must treat your guests to wonderful linens too. Make sure the guests sheets are ironed!

We can't close this topic of linens without discussing "thread count." Thread count simply refers to the number of threads, both vertically and horizontally, in a one inch square of fabric. Using finer threads also allows for more thread per square inch. Finer threads often result in smoother, softer fabrics but can be more fragile. While we all like to brag about the thread count in the sheets, remember that how the cotton is treated can be a more important factor, i.e. as they do with the Pratesi brand in purchasing cotton from southern Egypt. Anything above 180 is totally acceptable while over 400 thread count is considered by some to be simply extraneous. We'll let you be the judge of how it feels to your skin. Maybe you need a 650 count to be comfortable? We prefer that at SOF!

Lastly, recently a new type of bed sheet has come out. Bamboo. Yes, really. We too were surprised but these sheets are advertised to be as gentle as silk. Their claim to fame is that they are breathable, helping you to stay cool in the summer and warmer in the winter. They are allegedly highly anti-bacterial and hypoallergenic. For our older SOF readers they are supposed to be very helpful if you have menopausal symptoms. Frankly, we think they would be great for him and her since one person is usually hotter or colder than their partner. Sounds like a plan to us for a good night's sleep. There are also Bamboo blankets and even Bamboo yarn to knit with. Try them out, students, and let us know what you think about bamboo for your bedding.

****

SOF would like you to be familiar with some terminology so when you are shopping you will sound well-heeled, as in affluent, students. Also, for those young SOF students who have a job in a large department store you will not look like a doofus if someone asks you if you have any of the following products:

Matelassé bed shams, coverlets, throws or bed shirts: Matelassé in French means padded or cushioned. Simply put the fabric pattern stands out with an embossed look.

Merino Wool throws: Merino wool originated in Spain. The flocks of sheep were controlled by the King of Spain and only were exported as a royal gift. The largest flocks are now in Australia. Know that this wool is prized for its soft and silky texture.

Muga Silk: It is a rare wild silk, spun from the cocoons of silk moths that live in the forest of Assam, which is in a small area in northeastern India. It is an uneven fabric renowned for its spun gold color and glossy texture. Only Kings and noble families wore this beautiful material. Anichini is the first company to develop this fiber for the home.

European Square: A large 26" by 26" pillow usually used in sets of three across the back of a King size bed.

Neckroll: A decorative pillow for your bed or chair.

Duvet: A duvet is a bag filled with down, feathers, wool or natural stuffing to create a warm covering in place of a quilt or bedspread. Duvet is French for down, as in birds, students. A duvet always should have a cover that is washable. We might add here that there is nothing like snuggling up under your duvet on a cold afternoon for a quick nap. They are like a slice of heaven, so light, so warm and totally worth the money. We do love our duvet …

**** 

We need to talk now about sensuality and that sensuous touch. This is a delicate subject but if you have the big bucks there are a number of sex toys on the market for that very thing. Please do not let your children read any further. We are not making recommendations here but just reporting on what we have learned.

It has been reported that an Australian jeweler plans to make a $1 million vibrator. He is intending on only making 10 limited edition pieces out of smooth platinum, each encrusted with 1,500 white diamonds. He has previously designed a $38,000 platinum dildo with 400 pave-set diamonds and a handle made out of conkerberry wood which is a rare timber from Australia. Another model is molded out of white gold that is studded with diamonds and is completed with one large white pearl on the top for $8,000. It comes with matching earrings and a necklace. Veeery interesting, again we make no moral judgments or recommendations. All we are interested in is your happiness, students, however odd that may be.

**** 

One last word; we need only look at some exclusive private schools to see that the inbreeding in some affluent suburbs and cities is getting out of hand. Please students, branch out! If you don't believe this, you have only to attend a local Polo Match for proof! There is nothing wrong with adding some new blood to the family tree. If you've just won The Power Ball Lottery and are new to the Polo Groupies, take heart, they might just need your lineage to survive!

## Lesson Fifteen Quiz

1. Which of the following should be a staple of your boudoir?
    a. Feather Pillows
    b. 650 Thread count Sheets
    c. Soothing Music
    d. Champagne, e.g., Dom Perignon, Crystal, Ace of Spades or personal preference
    e. All of the above

ANSWER: E – If you couldn't answer this simplest of questions please go back to the beginning of this lesson and start underlining with your yellow marker!

2. Who or what is Pratesi?
    a. A Famous Artist of the 18th Century
    b. Fine Linen Merchant
    c. Neo Classic Line of Furniture
    d. Oprah's Hairdresser

ANSWER: B

3. When and where should you meet your lover/spouse?
    a. At Home
    b. A Fine Hotel Establishment
    c. Drive-In
    d. No Tell Motel
    e. A & B

ANSWER: E – Thread Count, People, Thread Count!!

4. What is diluting the Upper Crust of Society?
    a. Dot com millionaires
    b. In-breeding of the Affluent
    c. High waters of Lake Superior
    d. Facebook
    e. Royalty marrying Royalty
    f. B & E

ANSWER: F

5. Where did Merino wool originate?
    a. San Merino, CA
    b. San Salvidor
    c. Australia
    d. Spain

ANSWER: D – Kind of a tricky question to see if you were paying attention. Merino wool originated in Spain, but now is found mainly in Australia.

6. How much should you pay for sex toys?
    a. Whatever it takes to make you happy or your partner
    b. Don't ask, don't tell
    c. Does that include matching earrings and a necklace?
    d. We don't care!

ANSWER: D

7. What couple is the greatest love story of modern times?
    a. Brad and Angelina
    b. Elizabeth Taylor and Richard Burton
    c. The Duke and Duchess of Windsor

d. Mickey and Minnie
e. Heidi Montag and Spencer Pratt

ANSWER: C – Like them or not, when a man will abdicate his throne for you, move to another country and then buy you the most outstanding collection of jewels at that time, which would eventually be sold at a major auction house after both of your deaths, that surely is the greatest love story of modern times.

# LESSON SIXTEEN:
## Our Pets
"Never a Bowl of Fish! Have an Aquarium!"


NEED WE GO any further than the above statement?

> Not a mixed breed, a Show Dog.
> Not just a horse, but a Hunter-Jumper.
> Not a tom cat, but a Siamese.
> Not a parakeet, a pair of Finches.

If one of the "Nots" has stolen your heart, at least give him or her a regal name. Please no Spot, Shadow, Elvis or Bingo. Try a little elegance such as: Natasha, Kingsley or Mavis Astor. We particularly like Mavis Astor since she is a Yorkie who lives on the Gold Coast in Chicago but then we digress.

If your small child or grandchild should come up with one of those unfortunately common names you might be stuck. Your friends may consider you quaint or old fashioned, but if someone is new to your home and you are introducing your pet, you might add here that the children named it and you rescued it! Save some face, students. Remember, everyone always thinks highly of someone who rescues those poor, unfortunate animals. Frankly, it is beyond us how anyone could dump their dog or cat which has done nothing but love you. These people will never be SOF material. Maybe some jail time might improve their attitude toward man's best friend. Think football player, seems he has a new attitude toward dogs. But we will get off of our soap box, for we think you know where we stand on this topic.

Continuing on, students, always be sure your pet has the finest in cages, collars, leashes, tanks, and beds. Speaking of bedding, most of our little darlings manage to end up as permanent house guests. As well they should. How depressing to see some poor bedraggled dog or cat, hovering near the back door on a rainy night! Shame on you, students, if you ever put man's best friend through such an indignity! Oh, here we go again, we'll stop.

Now you have only to visit your local Pet Boutique to avail yourself of the latest and greatest in pet accoutrements … sparing no expense, of course. Remember, you will be judged on the sidewalks and dog runs with your charges. Make sure both of you look as stylish and befitting as one of your stature should. Think of riding the elevator with a wet, bedraggled hound, it is such a downer. If they had been wearing a cute jacket and booties this would not have been an issue. But just in case you were caught in an unexpected downpour, have your staff at the ready with warm towels; not only for you, students, but have the doggies get the needed rub downs, too.

**Flaunt Flash News**: … think Manfred of Sweden for your next little or big 4-legged beasties! A £12,000 jacket at Harrods for the dog that has everything was made out of Swarovski crystals and hand embroidered. This little number only took three weeks to make. No, we are not making this up, but the unfortunate news is, it was the perfect size for a Chihuahua. Guesstamation for a St. Bernard is approximately £150,000 and obviously it would take more than three weeks to make. Believe it or not, there are probably some people who would pay that. But if you are thinking something more reasonable, Manfred does also make a gold quilted jacket, fox terrier size, for approximately £399. Trés chic puppies here they come!

Okay, we can now hear you all complaining about the cost for a dog jacket. Check out a Burberry "inspired" trench coat with a hoodie.

Inspired is the operative term here. Burberry does not make clothes for dogs. They really should, they could make another fortune, but that is for a future discussion. There are maufacturers who do copy the Burberry tartan tan plaid and make adorable dog jackets, so check them out. We at SOF do not have a problem with our dogs wearing copies of signature clothes. Who's to know, and the dog is not telling either!

Speaking of copies, there are "inspired" collars and leashes that have LV, as in Louis Vuiton, printed on the leather. Don't like that, well they also have "inspired" Gucci and Burberry. Then you can have something plainer in a leather collar and add a Coach perfume bottle as a pet charm to it. Frankly, we don't know how they aren't sued for all of this copying but that is not our problem nor yours.

Now, speaking about collars, we do put our seal of approval on a little diamond-encrusted bell on a snake skin collar for your feline friends. You are saying to yourself now, "That is ridiculous, how over the top!" Rest assured, students, it does happen every day. Lastly, we are not into rhinestone collars but there are some fun varieties of collars and leashes with them so we will acquiesce. Think Afghan hound stylish or Bulldog fun!

**Flaunt Flash Fun**: Have a Birthday party for your favorite canine replete with cake and invite his or her friends and of course the owners. Party favors for all to take home can be "inspired" collars and leashes, homemade dog cookies and toys, all presented in a cute bag. What a fun day for all! Again another little social coup for you. Need we remind you that a caterer for this affair will make it ever so much more enjoyable for you? Check out our Pet Wear for the SOF Dog: www.schoolofflaunt.com Products

**Note**: Do not invite anyone who has a history of biting. That goes for the dogs as well as the humans!

But let's return to the topic of clothes. We at the School of Flaunt do not recommend outfits for our pets, e.g., a Sailor Suit or some other

Halloween type getup unless it is Halloween and you are out trick or treating with your children. Then we will make an exception. Lastly for your canines with either long ears or lots of hair, e.g., Afghan Hound, Cocker Spaniel etc., there are Snoods made for them. Gold Lamé is nice! What is a snood? Oh students, it is a stocking that is placed over the dog's muzzle and then goes past their eyes and pulls back their ears. Totally needed to keep food and water out of your babies' faces when they are eating.

Don't forget your designer should coordinate the little Prince's or Princess's bed and bedding with your rooms. Ditto with bowls, collars, leashes, etc. No old pieces of carpeting or rags for a resting spot. Really, how tacky!

Continuing on: cleanliness. You would think that we would not have to bring this up but, alas, we have found it to be. Students, this is of the utmost importance for all our darling little animal friends. No odors, please! There is nothing quite so awful as to pet your friend's dog and then two minutes later, as you pick up your glass of champagne, you find the odor of the dog is clashing with your perfume that you just spent $350 per ounce on. (JAR again, students.) You might not realize this, but show dogs are actually bathed and groomed once a week. No, it does not ruin their skin! We at the School of Flaunt can attest to this since we have shown dogs. Our 4-legged babies got a bath every week of their lives. No, we are not kidding! Did you ever see a mat, flea, tick or dandruff flake on one of our canines? We think not!

Watch the Westminster Kennel Show, or better yet, go to NYC to the show, and see how those Champions are treated. Plus, this is a wonderful way to acquaint yourself with many breeds of dogs and the very best in the U.S.A. If you decide to purchase one later, then their lineage will be something that you can proudly display along with hopefully a few ribbons that your new little "beasty" has brought home, too. We do highly recommend the Westminster Kennel Club Show and also Crufts in London, which is the British version of our Westminster, as places to start your research to buy that next champion or family pet. Plus if you decide to go to either, they do make for a nice little quick vacation. New York City or London? Maybe both? Remember to let the Mayor of NYC and the Queen know you will be there. Cocktails and dinner together?

If you do attend an AKC show (American Kennel Club) and get bit by the bug to show, we might as well tell you now that this is one of the most political games that you can play. The only way to win at this game is to have a "superb" dog if you are planning on showing it yourself, or pay the "big bucks" for a professional handler.

Now, let's say you want to buy that really wonderful puppy who will be a champion. Most of the top breeders have a waiting list a mile long. How do you get to the top of this list when you are a virtual nobody in the dog showing world? Well, now you are saying to yourself, "I can pay more so they'll move me up on their list." Possibly ... but we seriously doubt it, since most top breeders do want their little, potential, new champions to go to special homes where they will be "shown" and pampered, too.

Students be forewarned: you must get ready now, as the time has come for you to use those wonderful manners that we spoke about in Lesson Six. Trust us here, you will have your first conversation or "interview" by phone with that top breeder. Why, you ask? Because they won't have the time to talk with you at a show, "if" they are even there. Why? Puh-leese, because they are usually surrounded by their entourage of handlers * and friends. They do not have time for every Tom, Dick and Harry who wants to tell them how they just love their dogs. They have heard that a million times! But usually they do have rather large egos so make that statement on the phone. A little flattery never hurts.

*Note: Handler is a person who is paid handsomely to take your dogs to a show and handle them in the ring. They are expensive but worth it for a quick road to a championship for your dogs and then hopefully many BIS (Best in Show) wins, too. If you hear the term Best in Show wins, as in multiple remember that, this is the person you want to hire.

So now you make the first call; plan on spending at the very least 30 minutes talking with them. Hopefully you will be invited to their kennel for a second interview. If you are invited be prepared though because you will not see any dogs unless you "pass" this second interview. You will be kindly ushered to the door with a goodbye sounding something like this, "We'll be back to you when we have a puppy available." Consider that the kiss of death!

Continuing on: you will definitely be asked for references, if you have owned a dog before, are you planning on showing, or do you want just a "pet" quality puppy. If you are planning on showing they will want to know what you do for a living, e.g., can you afford it and will you take the time to do it. This is not a step to be taken lightly. Showing is time-consuming and expensive. If you have made the grade, at this point they will ask you for a hefty deposit! Gladly get out the check book and write the check immediately, before they change their mind.

A small word of advice, students. Make sure, when you are paying the big bucks for that show quality animal, that the pedigree is or at the very least 90% Champions for four generations back. Your breeder will have the appropriate AKC official pedigree for you to view. Having a Westminster Best in Show relative somewhere in that pedigree is also good! If this breeder is top-notch they probably will also be written up in their respective breed books. Check out those books for more information. We have never, and we stress here never, seen a top breeder advertise in the classified section of a newspaper. NEVER! So don't even go there! Fifteen hundred dollars for someone's back yard breeding. We don't think so.

Here is another insider's tip: if your breeder has the Dog (correct word for a male dog) flown in, for a breeding with one of their Champion Bitches (Bitch is the correct word for a female canine) then you know that they carry real clout in the showing and breeding of top animals. BUY FROM THEM ASAP! This is not the norm. Usually the Bitch goes to the Dog. Get used to the terms Bitch and Dog, that is the common vernacular in the dog showing world. We know, Bitch is hard on the ears at first but it is what it is. The lingo in the dog showing world.

Students, do be prepared to wait for that puppy and always be polite and charming when you are dealing with that Top Breeder of your potential new champion. You want to move your way up that list since they are not a puppy mill which has hundreds of puppies a year to choose from. Once you get your new baby remember only the best will do for him or her. Lastly, follow your breeder's advice when they tell you what judges to show under. Remember politics! They will usually be making a few phone calls to selected judges telling them about their latest and greatest new canine out there.

So you are thinking I just don't have the time and would prefer to merely display the trophies and ribbons from those Best in Show (BIS) wins. So simple, as we said earlier, hire a professional handler! Costly but usually quite productive. Your trophy case will overfloweth.

Lastly, be prepared to drop some money into advertising. Yes, you read right, every breed has their own magazine and then there are the all breed publications. Full page ads only! No half page or quarter page ads for you, speaks cheap to the other readers and judges who peruse these magazines. And you thought getting your child into a private school was hard. Welcome to the world of showing.

**** 

For those of you who prefer your Flaunt Feline beauties, you too should go to New York City to the Cat Fanciers Association— Iams Cat Championship, which is held each year at Madison Square Gardens. This is the cat version of Westminster. Check out some of these fine specimens that could eventually be sauntering around your home because anyone who has ever owned a cat will tell you, they own the home and are merely letting you reside there. Some gorgeous felines to consider are the Bombay, Burmese, Himalayan, Siberian and Thai breeds. (Please consult Lesson Eleven for more information on Hobbies Worth Your Worth.)

Finishing thoughts on cleanliness; do you really want your guests to sit down on a chair or couch that has animal hairs all over it, leaving these as souvenirs on their clothes when they get up? We implore you, visit the groomer frequently, board at only the best facilities and do find the best veterinarian in town. Which reminds us, when traveling with your four-legged babies, the Four Seasons has a Puppy Menu and they do have room service 24 hours a day. Dog walking and games are also available.

****

Students, proceeding merrily along with our pets remember we said, never a horse have a Hunter-Jumper. Picture little Tommie or Tammie in that cute outfit, replete with riding hat, jacket and $400 boots participating at Pony Club events. How could you not buy them a wonderful horse? For those of you who don't know, Pony Club is a must for new riders. You learn all of the disciplines for eventing, English competition and how to take care of your animal. But, let's face the cruel hard facts, you have to start young, work hard, have good political connections and money to burn. Like dog showing, there are politics in this game, too.

The money aspect is the most important! Why? Because if your child shows any talent for the sport they will want to participate in show jumping, eventing and dressage. Prize money at these events is sometimes awarded but, usually, at the amateur levels, you will be lucky to cover any expenses. And, trust us on this, there are many. The top trainers are expensive, getting your horse to the prestigious events such as the Washington International Horse Show in Washington, D.C., or flying over to Dublin as in Ireland to compete requires a hefty bank account. But, again, trophies, medals and ribbons, besides beautiful pictures of your children flying over a jump are nice to display. And it is fun to take someone out to the stables and let them admire your beauties. Flaunt Fabulous there!

Now we want you to remember this. What is the Fédération Equestre Internationale or commonly known as FEI (English: the International Federation for Equestrian Sports)? It is the international governing body of equestrian (horse) sports. Where is it located? Lausanne, Switzerland. Repeat: FEI, FEI, FEI. If you hear the term FEI you won't be standing there with a blank stare on your face, will you? As for some flaunt talk you can mention that HRH Princess Haya Bint Al Hussein became their 13th president in 2006. She is an avid horsewoman and participated in the 2000 Summer Olympics representing Jordan. She is married to HH Sheikh Mohammed bin Rashid Al Maktoum, ruler of Dubai and is his junior wife. Now that is a little morsel of info that is good for cocktail chatter.

And last but not least, if you ever meet Eugene R. Mische, show respect! He was the greatest driving force and promoter of show jumping in the United States. His vision to make horse shows a spectator event has turned them into world class competitions that are sponsored by the likes of Budweiser, Rolex and Mercedes. His Cosequin Winter Equestrian Festival has grown to be the world's largest horse show circuit lasting 10 weeks.

So get ready to spend the really big money here but it will be worth the ride! You will be mingling with the elite, traveling the world and making contacts that will prove to be invaluable in the future. Tally-ho, as they say in England!

**** 

We are hearing some of you say right now, but I'm not really an animal lover. We, at the School of Flaunt, are but that is beside the point. What to do, what to do? We have the perfect answer for you. The six figure Fish Tank, as in 6 figures to have one installed! A mere 14 1/2 ft long, 450 gallon tank filled with exotics from the sea. Gorgeous! Think Jellies, Koi, Black Tang or even a pet Shark swimming in your home for your private enjoyment! Let your imagination go wild. No tacky, plastic, little mermaids or artificial plants for our SOF devotees' tanks. Fill those tanks with minerals for that perfect fish environment. Yes big chunks of beautiful minerals that they can swim around. This is true SOF at its best.

Think coming home in the evening and relaxing in front of your aquarium after a long day. So it cost $50,000 to install and $1,000 a month for maintenance before buying your fish. Who cares? Your body and mind will thank you for this. No more trips for Valium. Just sit down in front of that FANTASY FLAUNT tank and let your cares drift away. Now breath deeply and relax. Aren't you feeling better just thinking about this?

Here are some wonderful ideas for where those "Flaunty Fish" might reside: how about suspending the tank from the ceiling? This could make for a wonderful room divider. Or then there is the tank that is built above your bathroom tub. Ah yes, you lying in your tub reminiscing about your last vacation in the Bahamas scuba diving with those lovely fish swimming above you. Possibly a mega-tank in your game room by the pool table or even built into the floor. Large enough for personal diving experience? Love that idea! Or maybe just a smaller tank in your study going around all four sides of the room? Nothing is outside the realm of custom design. Remember, this can be considered therapy for one and all! Just a small suggestion: if you are living in an apartment make sure the base is properly reinforced. Horrors if hundreds of gallons of water destroyed the apartment below you. Now, fill your freezers with some brine shrimp and silver-sides for your exotics to have for a fine dining experience and you are good to go. Flaunt Fish at their best!

****

Lastly, we don't want to forget our feathered friends, Finches. Such lovely little creatures and so sweet. A pair is doable but think long and hard before you purchase a larger bird. Why? First of all, they can be noisy and messy. Sorry, but their feathers and food do tend to fly around. Bad pun we know. If you are residing in a New York City apartment, be prepared to have your neighbors complain to the super about the noise. But having said this, your exotic birds from the Parrot family are beautiful and can be part of your family for 50 years.

**Note**: Make sure they are taken care of in the will. They could outlast you!

Lastly, as long as you have good staff that will make sure your feathered friends are cared for, then buy the best in cages and display them proudly. We suggest that you teach those Parrots to say, "I love the School of Flaunt." We do so love that! Think Blue Mutation Amazon for $18,000 to $20,000. Now that is Flying Flaunt!

****

We must mention the following before we close the Lesson on pets. Our children sometimes request hamsters, snakes, reptiles and mice. We do want them to appreciate all of Mother Nature's creatures but please, and we are begging you, students, do make sure they are caged properly. Picture this: you are having a fine dining experience with your Senator and his wife plus a few other notables and then all of a sudden a small head appears at the end of the table. Shrieking starts, guests climb on their chairs, wine glasses fall over and the food gets cold! This is not a SOF affair. You will laugh about it in the future but believe us, no one wants to see anything "slithering" around your dining room! They won't be back!

As noted earlier: one final thought for your pets in the case of your sudden demise, (consult Lesson Fifteen on Amour), in your last will and testament make certain continued love and care is provided for your prized pets! They will thank you after you're gone.

**Flaunt Fiscal Tip**: Adopt a loving pet from the Humane Society. Treat that little dumpling as your baby! You will be the recipient of so much unconditional LOVE. This is the ultimate in the SOF life.

# Lesson Sixteen Quiz

1. What should you consider when purchasing a dog?
    a. Lineage, 90% of his background should be champions
    b. His or her color coordination with your décor
    c. Will the dog be compatible with your young children?
    d. Does the dog like your husband, wife, or partner?
    e. A, B, C

ANSWER: E – We know you will work out this little problem in D.


2. Not having the proper leashes, collars, and bedding for your pet can
   be equated with:
    a. Blue eye shadow and ratting your own hair
    b. Bumper stickers for your car
    c. Tacky, Tacky, Tacky
    d. All of the above

ANSWER: D


3. What is necessary for your pet's protection?
    a. Inoculations on a regular basis
    b. Rubber booties for snow and rain
    c. Documented Dog Walker with references
    d. Provisions in your Will for future care
    e. All of the above

ANSWER: E


4. True or False: Not all pedigreed animals are show animals.

ANSWER: True – Didn't we tell you that you should only purchase from a long-time breeder who preferably has many Best in Show winners to brag about? Go back and read this lesson again if you answered false! You are the idiot who pays the back yard breeder $1,500 for a "questionable" pure-bred pooch!

5. Toeing out, undershot or overshot bites, no depth in brisket, hocking in. What do these mean?

ANSWER: Yikes! Any of these confirmation flaws should make you scream PET! We told you to do your homework and know what true great confirmation is. These are all terms that you never want to hear about your purebred dog. Now go get some books about confirmation and bone up before you go talk with that top-notch breeder and embarrass yourself!

6. How much should one spend on one's pet?

If you did not answer, "Money is no object!" you are not WORTHY.

7. What is the Humane Society?
   a. A Bunch of "Really Nice Babes"
   b. Cloning Company of America
   c. Angels who save stray dogs and cats
   d. Secret Society of the Ivy's

ANSWER: C

8. Should you adopt from the ASPCA?
   a. Yes, if you are a large donor/supporter
   b. Yes, if you want to save animals lives

    c. Yes, if the shelter is not a no kill

    d. Yes, if you want to not wait to get a companion

ANSWER: All of the above!

9. The FEI was formed in 1921. How many national organizations are now affiliated with the FEI?

    a. 13

    b. 52

    c. 134

ANSWER: C – This is why we always need to be doing our research, students. The answer was not in our book.

Now for extra credit memorize these names: HRH Bernard, Prince of the Netherlands; HRH Prince Philip, Duke of Edinburgh: HRH the Princess Royal; HRH La Infanta Pilar, Duchess of Badajoz and HRH Princess Haya Bint Al Hussein. Why? Because they are the last five Presidents of the FEI. You need to know these things! How embarrassing if you are fortunate enough to meet any of them or their families and don't even recognize their names. Trés tacky! FLAUNT FAILURE!!

10. What is a must for your custom fish tank?

    a. Lighting for the tank that can be controlled for different colors

    b. Plastic Mermaids

    c. Plastic plants

    d. Plastic Gold Fish

ANSWER: A – Have we taught you nothing in Sixteen Lessons, students? We hate plastic. Surely you remember that. We are breathing deeply now and thinking of going home to relax in front of our fish tank and not think about you anymore!

## LESSON SEVENTEEN:
## SOF WOMB TO TOMB

"Milestones: Baptisms, Bar & Bat Mitzvahs,
Debutante Balls, Weddings, & Funerals"

WHEN YOUR CHILDREN enter this world, if you are of a religious faith, a Baptism or Welcoming Party is a must! Not only are you announcing to the world a probable President of the United States or that the next CEO of Microsoft has arrived, but it is just sooooo socially irresistible not to have a party for the little darling afterwards!

We would suggest a tea dance with the baby present for the receiving line and then his or her Nanny can take the baby home. Remember the little darling will get tired and frankly there is nothing more annoying than a tired, cranky baby or possibly a 3 year old. Meanwhile Mommy and Daddy can bask in the limelight, sip some bubbly and mingle with their guests. A small aside here, this is a great way to start the family history with photos placed in sterling silver frames that can be passed down for generations to come. May we also add that a small oil painting of the baby would be lovely too, but please, students, do not, and we repeat "do not" line the walls of your hallways with "photos" of the children. Yes, you can you have a number of photos on top of your baby grand piano in the formal living room or in your study on the book shelves but never lining the walls! Terribly declassé and please, if you are doing a video this is not the time to experiment with amateurs. Your neighbor's child might be adorable, your brother-in-law clever with a camera, but remember, we are creating history here.

Normally these events are strictly for the family and a number of close friends. So as for keeping the peace, so to speak, if you want to have them bring their children, please have a separate room for the children to eat in and also be entertained. Remember the adults are sipping the bubbly, eating caviar on blinis, engaging in pleasant conversation, listening to some wonderful music from a harpist and possibly enjoying your gardens. The children should be playing games, eating chicken nuggets and fries and chasing one another around in a far-away room. Not that we don't like children, but there are times when "they do not need to be seen or heard," a quote from Lady Beatrice Beegleman. We wish we had a dollar for every time our parents brought up Ms. Beegleman's mantra.

Now this is where the children can be seen and heard: birthday parties, bar and bat mitzvahs, and graduation affairs. Then, as they become older you can move them up to deb parties and an engagement party. Hopefully by the Deb and Engagement parties, you have sound, lovely young adults. If not, definitely reconsider. More information can be found in Lesson 5 on entertaining and children's birthday parties, but we digress here and want to return to "milestones" in your lives.

**** 

A bar or bat mitzvah is about the coming of age of a Jewish boy or girl at thirteen. It is a celebration of that moment when the parents are accepting that their children are growing up. Today these parties have become total extravaganzas for this rite of passage. A bare minimum of $50,000 to $100,000 is not uncommon to be spent on one of these affairs since no longer are they a family dinner with a few cocktails. We are talking serious competitive events! Who can upstage and outdo the last person.

**Flaunt Flash Tip**: Try not to be the first to give your bar mitzvah for the season if at all possible. You know they will be watching and figuring out how they can best you! And if you are in the higher income tax bracket, remember millions have been spent by the well-to-do, to celebrate only "one" bar or bat mitzvah.

These are must haves e.g., a theme, "A" list rock stars and other entertainers, Cirque du Soleil, best caterer in the city, professional photographer (not your brother) and top-notch floral designer. Leave nothing to the imagination! Think about having this event at Yankee stadium or Radio City Music Hall. No we do not jest, it has been done!

The event should be replete with multiple appetizer stations scattered through the room since you do not want your guests to have to stand in long lines. As we have mentioned before SOF does hate lines of any kind! A given here is multiple bars and staff always at the ready with trays of champagne. Follow all of this with a sit-down dinner of four courses and this can easily run $300 to $400 per person. You must be prepared to wine and dine and entertain in a big way. Your reputation is on the line here!

So these affairs are over the top, you know and we know they are, but who cares? You are helping the local economy, students, and that is a good thing. Remember, you will be competing with dozens of these so have the pen poised over the check book and let no expense stop you. Surely you do want your children to know that you love them. We so love using guilt!

****

Ah, now one of our favorite milestones is the Debutante Ball. We know you are rolling your eyes here … stop because you are looking foolish. We're here to tell you that they are not dead but very much still alive. From New York City to Vienna, London, Paris and the Philippines. Even the movie stars want their daughters presented at debutante affairs. But lets continue on.

Modern-day balls are often huge charity events where the parents donate a certain amount of money to the designated cause and the "invited" guests pay for their tickets. Debutante balls are held in most major cities but are larger affairs in the South. Need we remind you of traditions and still needing to know how to curtsy? And puh-leese no polyester, which should be a given, and not too much cleavage. Chic haute couture, that is what we want for our School of Flaunt devotees' children. Nothing worse than a size 18 deb falling out of her dress!!

Cities like Dallas and Atlanta have multiple balls in a season. Yes, multiple and you better make sure that you and your offspring are invited to all! If you hear the term Idlewild Organization, The Dallas Symphony Orchestra Presentation Ball, or La Fiesta de las Seis Banderas, rest assured that all of these Debutante balls will benefit charities and it is important that you be seen there. Need we again remind you that charities, movers and shakers and your social status are all entwined?

You think this is not important? Well think again, your name should be on the list of invited guests for these balls. Besides being terribly chic, you might even run into some relatives of sitting Presidents. Perfect example of this: Lauren Bush, niece of President George W. Bush, made her debut in Paris. Heed our words of advice well, always be planning ahead, students, even though it might be for twenty years from now. Time flies!

We covered Dallas and Atlanta but let us not forget New Orleans where a debutante will usually have her coming out party during Mardi Gras season. Alternatively in the North a young woman has her coming out party given by her parents which can be held at any time during the year but usually is scheduled on her birthday. Chicago Deb Balls revolve around the Holidays. So, alas, it is very important to know the social scene where you live and in other parts of the country. Try not to limit your daughter's future to your home town. Branch out as if your family tree counted on it, because it just might!

**Flaunt Flash Tip**: In the South debutantes are referred to as Southern Belles. This is a necessary distinction to remember if you are from north of the Mason-Dixon line, never let them think you are just another Yankee. Do remember local etiquette!

We are positive you are now probably thinking we have forgotten, the big apple, New York City. Surely you do not believe that we at the School of Flaunt would not include the most renowned of these balls. You question what it is? It is the Viennese Opera Ball in New York City and it is an absolute must on your list to attend. It simply is! We will hear no excuses from you for not attending this annual charity gala.

This is the Grand Daddy or should we say Grand Dame of them all! Not only are there Dignitaries and Diplomats attending but the ball opens with Cadets from the U.S. Military Academy at West Point posting the flags. The debutantes (ages 16 to 25) are presented with their dance escorts (ages 18 to 30) along with their West Point Cadet escorts. Usually you will find not only the parents but the doting grandparents of the Debs in attendance with all of the guests. Then after the presentation of the Debs, all will dine on a four course sumptuous dinner, followed by dancing. A post Ball party from 1:00 to 4:00 AM for the younger crowd, which includes a full buffet supper, ends the evening.

Please remember to have your limo back in place to drive everyone home or back to their respective hotels if not staying at the Waldorf. A small point, do take off five pounds before this event. You will be more comfortable that evening in your gown or tuxedo. Think zippers and cummerbunds for they do not stretch.

One final note: The Viennese Opera Ball is one of the last to be considered a white tie and tailcoats affair, with the Ladies wearing floor length ball gowns and opera gloves. But don't think you can call up and just write the check for your daughter. Trust us, that will not happen! There is a recommendation committee that selects the debutantes and their male escorts. So start making friends in New York now. Time is of the essence here, for your daughter is getting older by the minute!

Lastly, you will need to make a suite reservation at the famed Waldorf Astoria Hotel in Manhattan where this ball is held. Oh the Waldorf, it is a great place to be seen and do some people watching still. If the Waldorf is booked don't fret, remember the name Trump. Book with the Donald. And before we forget, you will also have to be able to ballroom dance. Find a Dancing with the Stars pro and do take some lessons! Just call the Host, Tom Bergeron. His private number is listed in your cell phone? Isn't it? Consider putting him on speed dial. Remember, no break dancing, chest pumps or bootie bumps allowed. What happens in the wee hours of the morning we can not control!

So you still don't think people want to attend these affairs. We heartily disagree! The Paris Crillon Haute Couture Ball or Le Bal de Haute Couture, of which Kokichi Mikimoto (as in Pearls) is a patron, has a non-stop list of young Ladies who would like to be presented to society at this ball. All the Debs wear his jewelry and each debutante wears a couture gown made just for her. This outstanding event is held at the Hotel Crillon in Paris. From movie stars to politicians' daughters, they all want to attend. Even the daughters of ranking members of China's Communist party are attending now. Will wonders never cease! And remember we told you that these balls serve humanitarian purposes. This one helps the underprivileged in more than thirty countries. Did You Debut? Hope so!!

Finally, if riding that dirt bike and tossing down a few beers with your biking friends is still what you think is a chic affair then there is no help for you! Please put this book down and read no further. But for those of you who are still interested in learning how the other one percent does live, continue on.

****

What truly is the "pinnacle" of all parties and milestone events? The Wedding! Naturally this will be the wedding of the season and will be featured on the society pages of Town & Country.

**Flaunt Flash Tip:** Is the current *Editor of Town and Country* on your guest list? Hope so.

Get ready to cash in some CDs and sell some stocks. From ten bridesmaids, to valets for the reception, don't leave anything to chance! Keep the champagne flowing, bar open and the band playing.

**Flaunt Flash Tip**: Always have plenty of cash on hand for emergencies, for they can happen, e.g., you run out of champagne, cash talks, and they will deliver. Want the band to play a little longer, cash rules.

As for you brides … No Bride-zillas! Your parents have perfectly planned this event with your participation, so remain cool, calm and collected throughout. Choose your bridesmaids as if your life and social standing depends upon it. Trust us on this it probably really does!

Absolutely no high-maintenance friends in your bridal party. It is your day and you should be in the limelight, not one of your bridesmaids. Needless to say, never have a bridesmaid who you might find in the back room with a guest! You get the picture here? And lastly, no one who is going to show up with her new tattoos glowing in the dark! We shudder at that picture. In fact, screen all involved for tattoos. No exceptions and that goes for the bride too!

We know of one grandmother who fainted when her grandson's bride-to-be, started to walk down the aisle with a new brilliant tattoo on her left arm! Poor dear, when she came to, she kept mumbling something about being in Hell and had to be escorted from the church before the wedding started. And remember how hard you had to work to get Anna Wintour, the "Empress" of all fashionistas, to attend this wedding. Do you really think she would approve of the bride and the bridesmaids dressed in couture and then covered in tattoos? We think not and can hear her whispering under her breath, "truly tacky, so non-SOF!"

**Flaunt Flash Tip**: Make sure that your makeup artist, who will be doing the bride's and attendants' makeup, brings body makeup too. Just in case, you can then cover up any of those nasty tattoos that hadn't been previously discovered.

Think of having Trish McEvoy on stand by for makeup work. Better yet, hire her for the day! Ooops maybe not since she should be on your invitation list, so hire her assistant!

Continuing on, now lets talk about some really over-the-top wedding items. Starting with a wedding dress featuring 150 carats of diamonds valued at $12,000,000 or a wedding bouquet that is valued at $125,000 because it too has ninety gemstones, nine diamonds and a star-shaped ruby. Now that is way over the top!

Want to know what the most expensive wedding was? Lakshmi Mittal, who is the third richest man in the world, give or take, put on a $60,000,000 wedding for his daughter. Yes you did read right.

This wedding or some say, "coronation," because it outdid even the Royals, was held at the Vaux-le-Vicomte, a 17th century castle. The celebration lasted 6 days! For 60 mil it should have but whose counting? The wedding invitations were 20 pages in length, encased in silver and included verses written by family members. Only a mere 1,200 people were invited. Unbelievable, but true, students. Hope they stay together! Why do we see a pre-nup written before that wedding?

Then, of course, there are the totally out of control celebrity weddings that we all see in the tabloids and on TV. The good news is that they do sell pictures of the wedding and the proceeds go to their pet charities. Small point: of course, the selling of the rights to cover their weddings is also a good way to control the media feeding frenzy and then there is the charitable tax deduction. Working all the angles that is why they have managers and tax consultants. Work it, too, if you can, students.

Lest we forget, we need to talk about security. The White House needs to take advice from certain "A" List movie stars, who required all of their guests to arrive with their invites because the invitations had been embossed with holograms to stop crashers with dummied invitations. Helloooo White House and their security! Can you take a hint? Now, if you are having any type of large affair it might not be a bad idea for you, too. Unfortunately we have been to large galas where "lookie loos" just had to come inside and join the party. Then there are the proverbial professional wedding crashers, we don't want that for you!

Now where is the perfect place for the nuptials to be held? Castles seem to be a recurring theme with our celebs or there is the back yard wedding behind your parents 55,000 square foot home. At-home affairs, in estates, are popular now, too. Don't forget there is always a fireworks display to announce to the world the special union of the rich and famous.

Destination weddings have become the very "in" thing to do. Think Scotland, married in a castle, piped in and out for the ceremony. How much fun would that be? Lots! Of course, you must have everything already staged for your guests that have made the effort to fly in. Luxury buses not school buses, perish the thought, should be at the ready to whisk them to the affair and then back to the hotel. God forbid that you have a guest that imbibes a little too much and ends up in a Scottish jail cell. We feel a migraine coming on at just the thought of this nightmare.

What does SOF recommend for your dinner? It has to be memorable, no expense spared from appetizers to the cake. Open bars and waiters everywhere with champagne flowing. A sit down dinner with five courses, crowned at the end with a five tiered wedding cake! This is not a rubber chicken event! Remember what we said about the bar mitzvah, well it holds true here, too.

**Flaunt Flop:** Having the In and Out Burger truck cater your wedding is probably a bad idea.

Just to add a little pizazz, when the happy couple is leaving a daytime reception have white Doves released and rose petals in hand for the attendees to merrily toss at the newlyweds. Let's not do the bird seed thing. Do you really want it in you hair and clothes when you are leaving? Dreadful that one! Our lips instinctively just moved into a pout just thinking about it!

If you are having an evening wedding you may want to consider fireworks. You are as special as the celebs and after all it is only money! A great touch here is for all of your guests to be holding "sparklers" to light your way into your new future when you are leaving. Yes, we can see you now in your couture outfit, groom in his Bespoke suit, smiling and waving at the merry makers. Please do put us on the guest list!

Whew a lot of work for the wedding planner but isn't that what you are paying them for? Remember, you only hold a bash like this once. God forbid there is a divorce but if there is, please make the second, third or whatever number marriage you are on subdued and tasteful. Lastly, if this is not a first wedding don't ask for gifts and never and, we repeat, never, ask for money. We know in some cultures it is appropriate to give money, only then may you break our rule.

To give you some guidelines for a formal wedding with an evening reception for 300 here is what you might expect to spend: Religious Service and Officiate, $3,000; Bridal Gown and Headpiece, $25,000 (small suggestion: Contact Martin Katz & Renee Strauss for bridal couture, or Vera Wang and go to New York for private fittings), flowers, including personal, ceremony and reception, $40,000 (think that is high, rumor has it, the Donald's last marriage cost him $100,000 for the flowers alone), catering per person, $400, cake custom created just for you, $5000, live dance band, $20,000 plus, photography, $5,000, invitations for 300, $3,000 (you do want them to have the best paper and engraving). Anyway, these could be conservative estimates. Remember Elton John got $1,000,000 to perform at Rush Limbaugh's wedding. And now they are rumored to be great friends! We'd be his friend too for a million …

A small Flaunt point but ever so important: please remember that your flower girl is not an afterthought in today's wedding procession. She, too, must have some of the same color on her lovely little gown that will coordinate with the Bride's Maids. We don't want her to look like a Bride's Maid in miniature though, only to be color coordinated with them.

**Flaunt Flash News**: The new Duke and Duchess of Cambridge just staged the most elegant wedding of the decade! Not only being one of the most beautiful young women in the world, but the most elegant, too, from her dress, style, composure and most importantly her "cool stare" and "warm smile" for the cameras she will be unmatched in wedding history! Sister of the Bride, Pippa, was wonderfully understated as to not upstage the Bride. Remembering it is the Bride's day and not hers! Kudos to the Middletons for having such beautiful manners. They had to have made HRH very proud. Another event for the "Flaunt" history books.

**Flaunt Fiscal Tip**: Small, intimate weddings are some of the loveliest we, at the School of Flaunt, have attended. Think small and the bill will diminish! We know one couple who kept their wedding TOP SECRET … only the family in attendance. They sent out announcement cards and all their friends were thrilled for them. Note: If you get an announcement, it is your prerogative as to whether to send a gift.

****

Well, the children are married and you should be getting your house in order. Please always have the bills settled and trusts up to date. Remember, Funerals or Celebrations of Lives still need to be perfectly coordinated affairs. Yes, we said "affairs," since remember the movers and shakers in your community and hopefully even world wide will want to attend.

The cameras will be set up outside to take pictures of the mourners and family as they arrive so you need coordination inside and out. Think, a well oiled machine. If wise, you will make all decisions long before the inevitable! This is your final tribute and surely you want to have some input. Please remind your family they might need to have security at the funeral. You wouldn't want them to be blindsided by unwanted paparazzi or possibly a relative turning up who no one knew existed, if you get our drift. Think New York Times and these headlines: Mystery Child from Former Paramour Appears at Graveside. This certainly would put a sordid twist on an already sad state of affairs. Valium would be needed in a hurry for the family members.

**Flaunt Flash Tip**: Always have the family attorneys handy to handle any of these unforeseen incidences.

Alas, select a funeral home that can handle large groups and has the finest line of caskets. We recommend bronze or carved solid mahogany. Preferably your casket should be in a sea of white roses or orchids. A gorgeous scene even through all those mourners' tears. And lest you forget, remember always have a copper-lined vault to protect one and all!

**Flaunt Flash News**: The economy might have slowed down but not for the rich! Billionaire alert … you can now have a golden coffin equipped with a cell phone for a mere 280,000 euros. Now who you going to call? Ghost Busters? Sorry, probably poor humor but we just couldn't resist.

Puh-leese a phone in the coffin? Even we at SOF think that is ridiculous! Are you a Mummy, with a checkbook in hand, in that casket? Next thing we know you will have a pyramid built in which to be buried. Good luck with that idea.

So the Mummy idea is not appealing. Want cremation? No problem! Just retain the best. Do not go to Urn City to purchase your final resting place! No tacky, cheap, little urns for you. We had a close personal friend who told us that as her mother aged she would forget which urn held her husband's ashes and which one was the family dog. Which leads us to this question: Who did she love more, the dog or the husband, as both urns were approximately the same? We dare not go down that slippery slope.

Note: If considering Burial at Sea, preferably from a destroyer, this should never be a problem due to your political donations and connections. (Please see Lesson Ten regarding politics).

****

Mausoleums, grand mausoleums! Oh, they are so nice and your entire family can eventually rest in peace together. We would recommend that you overbuild. It is so hard to add on an addition to a mausoleum. We are thinking Mausoleum Nauseleum because of an addition.

Must haves: solid granite, plenty of marble, possibly a touch of gold, bronze doors and stained glass windows are all a must. Your final resting place should be as tasteful and beautiful as your every day life has been. In fact, why not have a party when construction is completed? Break a bottle of champagne over it and then go dancing. We love any excuse to have a party!

Views, views, views! You know from our previous Lessons how important School of Flaunt thinks views are when selecting property. This goes for selecting your final resting place, as well. We prefer the view or at least have a spot under a tree. (So good for photo-ops.)

If you are in doubt, please visit Woodlawn Cemetery in New York. It is the Park Avenue of cemeteries. Such noteworthy Industry Barons, as Astor, Borden, Woolworth and Westinghouse are in repose there. Take copious notes on the use of gargoyles and spires, research copies of chapels from Europe and tombs built like temples. This will help your architect when designing your mausoleum. Remember, you were a God or Goddess among mere mortals and the world will recognize this when they see your final resting place. We can feel ourselves tearing up at the very thought. Tissue please.

**** 

Grieving widows please remember, black, black, black and simple diamond jewelry. Always wear a black hat with veil and possibly a feather which will photograph nicely for the NY Times. In fact, all family members should be in black, except for children under 12. We hesitate, but must mention NO DENIM. The Club won't allow said dress for the reception afterwards.

We would think this is a given but those presenting eulogies must be family, or close personal friends. We know the staff loved you but this is not the time. Please, though, remember them in your will and invite them to the reading. They have been an integral part of your life!

A sordid story about eulogies: one grieving widow we knew, flew in a national news anchor and went on to tell how she had met him!

We heard you gasp, we did, too. This deceased husband deserved a great send off not a "babbling" widow. Please do "not" try to make your dear family member's funeral ABOUT YOU!!

A final suggestion: a nice fly-by tribute from the Blue Angels would be outstanding, or if well-timed, those white doves released at the end of the service. Do make sure they are trained, you wouldn't want any surprise droppings on your guests. Perish the thought! Note: No balloon releases. So yesterday!

Lastly, may we recommend a version of an Irish wake! Yes, no matter what your nationality or religion, it's a great escape for your loved ones and friends, stunned by your tragic end! Let the Jameson flow and visions of trust funds dance through their heads! You were a wonderful provider, to be sure!

# Lesson Seventeen Quiz

1. What three things do you need to make a Baptism complete?
    a. A Church
    b. A Baby
    c. A Tea Dance
    d. Baptismal Gown in rare Belgian Lace
    e. All of the above

ANSWER: E


2. Why do you want a Louis Vuitton Monogram Mini Lin at your baby's baptism?
    a. It is the diaper bag of all diaper bags
    b. Your Nanny should only have the best
    c. It includes a washable changing mat, address holder, key ring holder & two baby bottles
    d. It is so reasonable at $2,200 that everyone should have one
    e. All of the above

ANSWER: E – Now this has to be total flaunt!


3. What is the most important ingredient for a beautiful wedding?
    a. Love
    b. Caterers
    c. Bride and Groom

ANSWER: B

4. Which of the following should "nevah" be done at your daughter's wedding?
    a. The "Chicken Dance"
    b. Throwing the Bouquet!
    c. Best Man Toast

ANSWER: A – Please tell us you did not miss this one!


5. What was the Queen thinking of Princess' Beatrice and Eugenie fascinators at William and Kate's wedding?
    a. I will kill Fergie when I see her again.
    b. Thank you Lord for giving me the presence of mind not to have invited their mother!
    c. Where was their father when the decisions were being made as to what those two would wear?
    d. Off with all of their heads!
    e. I need my evening cocktail now!
    f. All of the above.

ANSWER: F – We feel for her Majesty, how many times can she be humiliated by her family?


6. Which of the following is unacceptable behavior at an Irish wake?
    a. Taking home movies
    b. Adult Beverages
    c. Dancing

ANSWER: A

7. Sketch your family mausoleum or grave site below:

8. Give yourself extra credits if you have your trusts in order.

## POSTSCRIPT AND NEXT STEPS

IN CLOSING, DEAR students, we do not want you to ever judge a book by its cover but unfortunately many in society do. Knowing this fact to be true we have tried to cover most aspects of a gracious life. Starting with something so simple as your wardrobe and manners, we have weaved our way through how old money lives and how you can emulate them. We've tried to give you a peek into the upper-crust and how easy it can be to learn savoir faire.

Our goal was to have you become sophisticated, poised and interesting to all. Remember, we do not want them to think of you as just a paperback book, no you are a beautiful leather-covered hardback. Otherwise thought of as special.

The old adage of treating others as you would like to be treated is our mantra and how we want you to live. Caring for our fellow human beings as well as the animal kingdom is a given, therefore we not only recommend that you give back, but act with a loving and caring attitude. Now you are truly School of Flaunt material.

Even if you are only of modest means remember our helpful hints, for they will surely open the doors of opportunity and possibilities for you. You never know when the right moment may come along for a little flaunt and you must always be ready! If you expand your horizons then the world is your oyster. New adventures and exciting friendships await you.

Now you exude savoir vivre and can mingle with the movers and shakers! So, dear students, enjoy knowing that you are on the right track in the fast lane. Ladies and gentlemen start that eco-friendly engine or the Lamborghini, for the race can be fast and furious, but ever so much fun!

Bon Appétit, Bon Voyage, Bonne Chance and Repondez s'il vous plait!!

And always remember our Motto: MAKE IT BIG, FLAUNT IT BIG!

Your Divas of Good Taste,

Alexandra Smythe and Cate Clarke

You now are a graduate of the School of Flaunt and, after reading this book, you qualify for your Graduation Diploma.

Go to: www.schoolofflaunt.com and click on PRODUCTS, to order your personal graduation diploma.

# Flaunt Glossary

Flaunt Flash
Flaunt Fabulous
Flaunt Fiasco
Flaunt Fly
Flaunt Free
Flaunt Fashion
Flaunt Fashion Victim
Flaunt File
Flaunt Field
Flaunt Find
Flaunt Fishing
Flaunt Flying
Flaunt Flyer
Flaunt Fame
Flaunt Finery
Flaunt Figure
Flaunt Fair
Flaunt Fairy
Flaunt Finger
Flaunt Film
Flaunt Famous
Flaunt Frugal
Flaunt Fashionista
Flaunt Flag
Flaunt Food
Flaunt Foodie
Flaunt Face
Flaunt Fresh
Flaunt Fabulousness
Flaunt Facetious
Flaunt Facet

Flaunt Facial
Flaunt Facility
Flaunt Faculty
Flaunt Fair
Flaunt Fairway
Flaunt Fair-mindedness
Flaunt Faithful
Flaunt Fake
Flaunt Falderal
Flaunt Fail
Flaunt Failure
Flaunt Festival
Flaunt Fall
Flaunt Fallacious
Flaunt Fallacy
Flaunt Fallen
Flaunt False
Flaunt Falsify
Flaunt Falter
Flaunt Familial
Flaunt Familiarity
Flaunt Famine
Flaunt Famish
Flaunt Fan
Flaunt Fanatical
Flaunt Fancy
Flaunt Fandango
Flaunt Fanfare
Flaunt Fan mail
Flaunt Far
Flaunt Farce
Flaunt Fare
Flaunt Farm
Flaunt Farce
Flaunt Fast

Flaunt Fat
Flaunt Fattening
Flaunt Fatal
Flaunt Fat cat
Flaunt Father
Flaunt Fatigue
Flaunt Fraud
Flaunt Favor
Flaunt Fave
Flaunt Favorite
Flaunt Fear
Flaunt Feast
Flaunt Feature
Flaunt Federal Offense
Flaunt Feeble
Flaunt Feed
Flaunt Feeling
Flaunt Feisty
Flaunt Feline
Flaunt Fellow
Flaunt Fellowship
Flaunt Felon
Flaunt Feminine
Flaunt Finagle
Flaunt Fertilizer
Flaunt Fester
Flaunt Festoon
Flaunt Fetish
Flaunt Feather
Flaunt Fever
Flaunt Field Day
Flaunt Fiction
Flaunt Fire
Flaunt Fight
Flaunt Figment

Flaunt Figure
Flaunt File
Flaunt Filibuster
Flaunt Fling
Flaunt Find
Flaunt Film
Flaunt Filter
Flaunt Final
Flaunt Finder
Flaunt Fine
Flaunt Finery
Flaunt Finger
Flaunt Finish
Flaunt Finishing School
Flaunt Flip
Flaunt First
Flaunt Fists
Flaunt Flirt
Flaunt Flair
Flaunt Fix
Flaunt Flag
Flaunt Flamboyance
Flaunt Flash
Flaunt Flat
Flaunt Flaw
Flaunt Flexible
Flaunt Fleur
Flaunt Flop
Flaunt Fauna
Flaunt Flounder
Flaunt Flow
Flaunt Flourish
Flaunt Floral
Flaunt Flower
Flaunt Fluid

Flaunt Flunky
Flaunt Fluster
Flaunt Flux
Flaunt Flying
Flaunt Focus
Flaunt Foil
Flaunt Foliage
Flaunt Fold
Flaunt Full
Flaunt Folly
Flaunt Fog
Flaunt Folklore
Flaunt Following
Flaunt Fondness
Flaunt Fool
Flaunt Foolproof
Flaunt Footwork
Flaunt Foray
Flaunt Forbid
Flaunt Foray
Flaunt Force
Flaunt Forecast
Flaunt Foreign
Flaunt Form
Flaunt Formality
Flaunt Forte'
Flaunt Forum
Flaunt Fortune
Flaunt Forward
Flaunt Fortitude
Flaunt Foul
Flaunt Frame
Flaunt Franchise
Flaunt Fraternity
Flaunt Fraud

Flaunt Freak
Flaunt Free
Flaunt Friend
Flaunt Fresh
Flaunt Friction
Flaunt Frock
Flaunt Frontier
Flaunt Frown
Flaunt Fruitcake
Flaunt Frump
Flaunt Frustration
Flaunt Fuel
Flaunt Full
Flaunt Fun
Flaunt Function
Flaunt Fund
Flaunt Funk
Flaunt Furniture
Flaunt Fury
Flaunt Fuss
Flaunt Future

(This page intentionally left blank)

# About the Illustrator

## Biography of Illustrator: Joel Woodard

Joel Woodard is an interior designer whose work has appeared in The New York Times, as well as Traditional Home, House Beautiful, Hamptons Cottages & Gardens, and House & Garden magazines. He has also appeared on Martha Stewart's "Morning Living" radio program on the Sirius Channel and his work has likewise been featured on NBC Television's LXTV "Open House."

After graduating with honors from The University of Alabama, Joel moved from Alabama to New York City to pursue a career as a fashion designer. With stints at Geoffrey Beene and Arnold Scaasi in his Fifth Avenue couture salon, Joel designed his own line of eveningwear, selling to such carriage trade retailers as Bergdorf Goodman, Saks Fifth Avenue, Barney's New York, Neiman Marcus and Giorgio Beverly Hills. Joel shuttered his ready-to-wear enterprise after several years to take a degree in interior design from The New York School of Interior Design.

During his career in interior design, Joel has enjoyed working in some of New York's most important residences and on some of the region's most prestigious showhouses, with the most recent being the Kips Bay Designer Showhouse 2009.

In addition to his interior design work, Joel also operates J Design Antiques Garden, a small shop in the village of Oldwick, New Jersey, where he sells a variety of antique furnishings, art and accessories for the home.

In 2009 Joel was asked by Mr. Albert Hadley, widely known as the "Dean of American Interior Design," and of the venerable interior design firm Parish Hadley, to serve as an independent design consultant.

Joel Woodard Interior Design LLC
www.joelwoodard.com
www.jdesignantiquesgarden.com

CPSIA information can be obtained at www.ICGtesting.com
Printed in the USA
LVOW042117071211

258363LV00002B/33/P

9 781937 387198